AF675259

MEN OF STEEL

#Military Leadership for India

Since time immemorial, leadership has charted the destinies of nations and organisations for better or worse. While the world has transformed in every conceivable way in the last one hundred years, the principles of leadership have stood the test of time.

The volatility and complexity of the regional and international environment are the new normal. This has necessitated a de novo examination of leadership challenges in the context of the VUCA environment and the digital revolution.

The 15 chapters which comprise this offering cover a wide canvas of the nuances and imperatives of leadership, matched with outstanding authors of proven credentials. The book, while being focussed on military leadership, should also appeal to a wider cross-section of academia, governance professionals, the corporate world and all other fields where leadership plays a defining role.

The Indian Armed Forces are the ultimate guarantors of the nation's security and well-being. How this instrument of last resort performs will be determined by the leadership that steers the organisation in peace and leads it in war. The concluding part of this book examines how to produce leaders who are steadfast and visionary, who will measure up to the highest standards of military skills, and who possess the strength of character and mental resilience to carry the burdens that modern warfare conditions impose.

MEN OF STEEL

#Military Leadership for India

Editors

AK Singh | Yash Mor

KNOWLEDGE WORLD

KW Publishers Pvt Ltd

New Delhi

Centre for Land Warfare Studies

Delhi Cantt

New Delhi

Reprint, 2026

The Centre for Land Warfare Studies (CLAWS), New Delhi, is an autonomous think tank dealing with contemporary issues of national security and conceptual aspects of land warfare, including conventional and sub-conventional conflicts and terrorism. CLAWS conducts research that is futuristic in outlook and policy-oriented in approach.

Centre for Land Warfare Studies
RPSO Complex, Parade Road, Delhi Cantt, New Delhi 110010
Tel: +91.11.25691308 **Fax:** +91.11.25692347
Email: landwarfare@gmail.com **Website:** www.claws.in
CLAWS Army No. 33098

Copyright © 2022, Centre for Land Warfare Studies

All rights reserved. No part of this publication may be reproduced, stored in a retrieval system, or transmitted in any form or by any means, electronic, mechanical, photocopying, recording or otherwise, without the prior written permission of the copyright owner.

Disclaimer: The contents of this book are based on the analysis of materials accessed from open sources and are the personal views of the author. The contents, therefore, may not be quoted or cited as representing the views or policy of the Government of India, or Integrated Headquarters of MoD (Army), or the Centre for Land Warfare Studies. Attributability of the contents lies purely with the Author(s).

ISBN 978-93-91490-18-8 Paperback
ISBN 978-93-91490-48-5 ebook

Published in India by Kalpana Shukla

KW Publishers Pvt Ltd
4676/21, First Floor, Ansari Road
Daryaganj, New Delhi 110002
Phone: +91 11 43528107
Marketing: kw@kwpub.in
Editorial: production@kwpub.in
Website: www.kwpub.in

Printed and Bound in India

The content of this book is the sole expression and opinion of its author(s), and not of the publishers. The publishers in no manner is liable for any opinion or views expressed by the author(s). While best efforts have been made in preparing the book, the publishers makes no representations or warranties of any kind and assumes no liabilities of any kind with respect to the accuracy or completeness of the content and specifically disclaims any implied warranties of merchantability or fitness of use of a particular purpose.

The publisher believes that the contents of this book do not violate any existing copyright/intellectual property of others in any manner whatsoever. However, in case any source has not been duly attributed, the publisher may be notified in writing for necessary action.

Contents

Foreword

It is with great pleasure that I pen the Foreword to this book on Leadership, entitled, "*Men of Steel #Military Leadership for India*", co-edited by Lt Gen AK Singh (Retd) and Major Gen (Dr.) Yash Mor (Retd).

Leadership is germane to any walk of life, but if there is one institution that is defined by leadership itself, it is, perhaps, the Armed Forces and within that larger frame—the Indian Army.

Leadership, for us, men and women in the Armed Forces, is ingrained into our very beings and souls, right from the time we step into the academies and is nurtured thereafter, through live, operational challenges and other mechanisms across the course of our professional careers. Leadership in the Army comes in varying forms and shades: there is combat leadership, leadership epitomised by the raw courage and valour that drives combat leaders to lead men into fire and make the supreme sacrifice; there is creative leadership that brings about organisational cohesion and precision, while ensuring combat delivery in the most daunting of circumstances; there is thought and technological leadership that shapes the intellectual outlook and cutting edge prowess of the Army; then, there is leadership that anticipates the futures and drives change, etc. In this age of great strategic competition and persistent conflict, leadership in each of these domains is equally salient; each needs to be cultivated and nurtured carefully.

It is when many of these diverse attributes fuse into a single persona that we see icons such as Thakur Nathu Singh, KM Cariappa, KS Thimayya, Sam Manekshaw, Arjan Singh, Harbaksh Singh, Krishnaswamy Sundarji, PS Bhagat, Zoru Bakshi, SK Sinha, Sagat Singh and Arun Prakash, to name just a few. If we study their lives and biographies carefully—we will be vastly enriched.

Even in hierarchical structures like the Indian Army, good leadership is about a certain 'sharafat' exemplified by an axiom which goes something like this: "In any hierarchy it is axiomatic that there will be a Senior and a Junior; The Senior, if he is a gentlemen, will never show it; the Junior, if he is a gentlemen, will never forget it." A cultural context that is self-driven, not one necessarily enforced by discipline and the fear of punishment, as is commonly believed. So, leadership by example and emulation, is something that we must try and develop.

Military leadership has many hues but in the ultimate sense, leadership is about common sense, earthy wisdom, a strong moral fibre and trust. It has been righty observed, "In an atmosphere of trust even silence is understood. When mistrust prevails, every word gets misunderstood."

Little wonder then, that leadership is so very challenging. All of us in uniform are imperfect human beings, but if we remain diligent observers and students of the craft of leadership, we shall emerge as better leaders.

That is what makes this book so salient. It provides many valuable insights into myriad facets of the leadership domain.

So read, absorb, enjoy, grow into good leaders and, most importantly, always practise what you preach.

Jai Hind!!

Place: Shimla
March 2022

Raj Shukla
Lieutenant General
GOC-in-C, ARTRAC

Editors

Lieutenant General **A K Singh,** PVSM, AVSM, SM, VSM (Retd), is an Advisor and Adjunct Faculty with O P Jindal Global University and a Distinguished Fellow with Centre for Land Warfare Studies (CLAWS). The General is the erstwhile Lt Governor of the Andaman & Nicobar Islands and Puducherry, Ex GOC-in-C Southern Command and has been an alumni of NDA, Staff College, Camberley, UK, Malinovsky Tank Academy, Moscow and the Higher Command and National Defence College courses in India. He is one of the few officers to have trained with both the NATO and Warsaw Pact at the height of the Cold War. Known for his high integrity and professionalism, the General is looked upon as a role model by large numbers in the Armed Forces. The General has commanded the 7th Cavalry, a T-90 Tank Brigade, an Armoured Division and the most powerful Strike 1 (Corps), and has the distinction of conceiving and executing some of the largest ever manoeuvres in recent times. He has teneted key operational appointments as Brigade Major of the Kargil Brigade, three appointments in Military Operations Directorate, headed the foreign division of the army and was also the Director General Perspective Planning, where he drew up the long-term perspective of the Indian Army. After a distinguished service in the Armed Forces, the General was entrusted with the responsibility of Lt Governor of A&N Islands in July 2013 and later concurrently assumed the charge of Lt Governor of Puducherry in July 2014, where he made a great difference with his unique qualities of head and heart. He has been a member of Prime Minister's Team India, as also a member of the National Development

Council and Inter-State Council. The General is a frequent speaker at defence and civil forums and also contributes to the print media. His first book as editor,' *Military Strategy for India in the 21st Century* was published in 2019. His recent book titled *Battle Ready in the 21st Century* was published in March 2021. His blog may be accessed at: http//ak7cav.in.

Major General (Dr.) **Yash Mor**, SM (Retd), was commissioned in the Brigade of the Guards in June 1985. He commanded 1 Guards, an independent Armed Brigade, and a strategic Sub Area in Ladakh. In addition to Staff College, Wellington, he is also a graduate of Command and Staff College, Mirpur, Dhaka, Bangladesh. He has the distinction of being one of the pioneers in the UN Peacekeeping operation in Mozambique in 1993-94. He has taken an active part in counter-insurgency operations in Punjab and J&K. Known in the army for his 'Small Team operations' in South Kashmir, he excelled at the unconventional approaches to fighting terrorism. He was awarded the Sena Medal and Chief of Army Staff Commendation while serving with 36 RR (Garh Rif). He has been an instructor at the Defence Services Staff College and Director in Strategic Planning Group of the Perspective Planning Directorate of the Indian Army.

He is an alumnus of the prestigious US-based think tank, The NESA Centre, Washington DC. He has an MPhil and PhD in Nuclear Doctrine and Strategy from Osmania University, Hyderabad. Post-retirement he is an active author, editor, Educator on Unacademy, and YouTuber. His writings have appeared in leading journals and web-based portals. He is the first Chief Executive Officer of Save the Himalayas.

Introduction

Leadership is a very intriguing theme. Improved education and awareness have caused a spectacular shift in our thinking and functioning, which has transcended the intricacy of human behaviour as never before. Leadership is also a natural phenomenon in our day-to-day life. It is related to the principle of gradation and hierarchy. Whenever a few individuals get together for a common purpose, more or less, a leader is born, who is one of the members of the group who demonstrates greater aptitude and starts striving harder than the rest for the achievement of the group goals. In this book, we have endeavoured to examine leadership nuances in the armed forces, across a wide spectrum of environments likely to be confronted while in service and beyond. This endeavour has been spurred by a realisation that there is a dearth of published work on such an important subject in India, with recourse mostly to books and experiences published abroad. We hope this offering will partly fill that void.

Amongst the many qualities and attributes of a successful leader, arguably the most significant ones are "**integrity, vision and communication**". Integrity allows trust to be established and inspires and reciprocates loyalty. The leader must also possess vision and clearly articulate the ways and the means to achieve it. In articulating the vision, he must ensure that his subordinates share the same vision, which invariably is linked to communication. **Even an extraordinary vision articulated by an inspirational leader is of little value if he is unable to communicate it** to those for whom it is intended.

Both contemporary and former senior officers have incessantly voiced their concern and discontent with the conventional mindset of many strategic and operational-level military officers. In their view, many senior leaders are guarded and lack **creativity and ingenuity to engage in the "out-of-the-box" thinking** required to fully understand the nuances and challenges posed by the changing character of war and related national security challenges. The imperceptible basis of this critique also raises pertinent questions about **whether the new dimension of warfare poses unique challenges for strategic leaders, or it more appropriately requires time tested leadership competencies, applied with more creativity and risk-taking.** The answers to these germane questions would seem to hold great significance with respect to the readiness of our politico-strategic leadership and the competencies needed for the fast emerging geostrategic environment. The current national security environment is at best uncertain, dynamic, unpredictable, and complex. This calls for an **astute capability in our politico-strategic-operational level leadership.**

The concepts of military leadership are so universal and powerful, that most civil organisations in the developed world have not only adopted these, but have gone a step further, in refining and harmonising them with emerging technologies to optimise the end effect. However, in India, we still work in stiff silos and cynicism about the other side has become a roadblock that is yet to be overcome.

Traditional military leadership is associated with strong self-confidence and powerful egotism. However, we should be able to distinguish as what may be viewed as resolute leadership, could also be called stubbornness; self-confidence perceived as arrogance, determination as ruthlessness and motivation as ambition. One of the flaws of a few senior leaders is that they demand obedience not only to their orders, but to their ideas as well. There are **certain senior leaders who have a compelling and a riveting vision for the organisation,** who are skilful, charismatic orators and tend to attract subordinates; they however lack empathy, which leads to an inability to tolerate dissent. Consequently, they tend to gravitate towards admirers which completely negates truthful feedback on their own performance. Certain leaders are visibly 'hierarchy savvy' who are overtly obsequious to directions from higher headquarters at the cost of peers and subordinates. Real excellence goes hand in hand with humility, **seemingly not so profound a leadership virtue,** which is equally relevant and important in the military, civil and political environments.

Given the nature of today's armed forces, combining diverse cultures and values on the one hand, whilst coping with increasing technological, social, and economic challenges on the other, the expectations of rank and file are rapidly changing. Hence, the role of the Junior Leaders becomes even more important, and the armed forces need to place greater emphasis on developing and empowering them. Increased education and awareness have also led to a **contraction of the capabilities and awareness between the leader and his subordinates**. Therefore, it is ever more significant and essential that the senior hierarchy actively involves the junior leaders in organisational processes, as with the passage of time, our future generations of potential leaders will emerge from this very pool. In today's complex battlefield environment, where directive style of leadership is a prerequisite, the competence and leadership potential of our junior leaders is an important indicator of the organisational effectiveness. **Directive leadership is all about quality leaders and quality subordinates, where there is no place for mediocrity.**

In any hierarchical organisation, at every stage we are **expected to be exceptional leaders of men as also good subordinates, without comprising the former.** However, as leaders rise in the hierarchy, certain individuals focus to only become exceptional subordinates to their bosses rather than being exceptional leaders for their men or team. Unfortunately, it is here that the senior leadership unwittingly contributes in creating an environment which produces subservient subordinates who are aligned to every thought process of their bosses rather than developing a personality of their own. Whilst such subordinates may climb the hierarchical ladder in peacetime, they are likely to falter in combat situations. Also, **being an exceptional leader of men, in no way inhibits anyone from being a good subordinate, as these are not mutually exclusive.**

In the armed forces, **trust** and **ownership** are key components towards mission accomplishment. Ownership and trust also go hand in hand; ownership not only for the direct responsibility, but even for those indirect things that may impact the mission and the end result. When you take charge as a leader, there is a reputation that precedes you. However, it's your day-to-day actions, especially when the chips are down that have a major impact. Your teammates are quick to notice: Are you self-oriented, or do you give priority to organisational objectives and the team; do you stand up and be counted in a crisis situation and for your decisions; and do you apply the same standards to yourself that you expect your subordinates to follow. The writing becomes clear on the wall.

All leaders have their own personal style. Some are authoritarian, some perhaps more laid-back, which does not necessarily vary in both the operational and non-operational environments. The distinction between those leaders who win willing obedience from their subordinates and colleagues, as compared to those who merely extract compliance from them out of fear or a grudging acceptance of the authority, is an apt example of the difference between a transformational and transactional leader.

The 15 chapters which comprise this offering have been carefully chosen to cover a wide canvas of the nuances and imperatives of leadership, and matched with outstanding authors of proven credentials, who have been leaders at varying levels. The book, while being focused on military leadership, should also appeal to a wider cross-section of academia, governance professionals, the corporate world and all other fields where leadership plays a defining role.

The Indian Armed Forces are the ultimate guarantors of the nation's security and well-being. How this instrument of last resort performs will be determined by the leadership that steers the organisation in peace and leads it in war. The concluding part of this book will examine how to produce **leaders who are steadfast and visionary, who will measure up to the highest standards of military skills that modern warfare demands, and who possess the strength of character and mental resilience to carry the burdens that modern warfare conditions impose.**

The editors take the opportunity to thank Director CLAWS, the authors, the publisher and their teams, who provided the encouragement and support to see this project through. **And finally the book is a tribute to all leaders past and present, and those to follow, who have made the Indian Armed Forces such a formidable organisation in the service of India.**

Editors

1

Strategic Leadership Imperatives

Role of Military Leaders in Defining and Enhancing National Security

AK Singh

Introduction

The concept of India has been marked by a high degree of cultural pluralism and the capacity to absorb outside influences over centuries. India's strategic culture has also been shaped by our geography, history, social structures and religious beliefs; a tradition of localism and particularism, and an insular and inward-looking focus remain predominant. Notwithstanding its ancient civilisation and inherited wisdom, India remains somewhat tentative and insecure about the use of power.[1]

In the process, our efforts to develop and shape an indigenous strategic identity have also been ad hoc and unstructured. After Independence, there was little structured strategic thinking and even then, in compartments. That India still doesn't have an officially articulated "National Security Strategy" is a telling commentary.

As India tries to define its place at the high table, in this quest, there are obligations and expectations. This requires strategic leadership of an exceptional calibre, both in the civil and military domain. This chapter will attempt to examine the "Strategic Leadership Imperatives" and the role of military leaders in defining and enhancing National Security. The contents of this chapter would remain equally applicable to strategic leadership in other spheres and institutions.

There are three levels of military leadership and this is recognised and practised the world over. Starting with the cutting edge or tactical level leadership, graduating to the operational level leaders, who are like the conductors of a symphony orchestra, harmonising various tactical operations to achieve the desired operational objective(s). At the apex level is the conceptual-strategic leadership, where you lay down the vision, define the future course, shape and harmonise both the internal and external environments and, without compromising on the core values, optimise the end state. However, in the 21st century, such clear-cut divisions have been somewhat diffused by the speed and span of communications, with tactical incidents having operational and even strategic ramifications.

National Security in the 21st Century

The concept of national security in the 21st century has undergone a profound change and has moved beyond the realms of physical security alone. National security today encompasses five determinants, i.e., political stability, economic and technological prowess, diplomatic and military strength, society empowerment and environmental protection. The competition is more in the economic and related spheres than in the military field. Comprehensive National Power (CNP) is the new determinant; "generally means the sum total of the powers or strengths of a country in economic, military affairs, science and technology, education and resources, and its influence. In short, CNP may be simply defined as the comprehensive capabilities of a country to pursue its strategic objectives."[2]

The other phenomenon that impacts National Security in the 21st century is the diminishing power of the state; however, the expectations from the state have not reduced, leading to extraordinary pulls and pressures. There has been a paradigm shift in the very character of conflict, and one could argue, even the enduring essence of the nature of war may be open to re-examination. Modern-day conflicts are not merely confined to states, but have expanded to include sub-nationalities, terrorists, insurgents, religious fanatics and ethnic interests. Conflict today encompasses sabotage, subversion, non-kinetic confrontation and traditional armed conflict in all its forms. Thus, the state's response needs to be balanced, inclusive and one that incorporates political, societal, economic and military measures.[3]

In view of the emerging environment, our strategic leadership will do well to move towards a favourable politico-strategic-military construct to facilitate the pursuance of our National Security objectives. In the prosecution of modern-day security challenges, if the instrument of force is to regain utility, India's politico-strategic-military construct and the pattern of civil-military relations must undergo concurrent change and reform.[4]

Role and Imperatives for Strategic Military Leadership

Leadership is important in all spheres; however, military leadership is critical, for the armed forces are the ultimate guarantors of our nation's security and well-being. How this instrument of last resort performs will be largely determined by the strategic and operational military leadership that steers the organisation in peace and leads it in war. Being so important to a nation's well-being, the grooming, selection, focus and conduct of such leaders assumes great importance. It is therefore apt that we look at the role and imperatives for strategic military leadership and in our context, it would be wise to include operational level leaders too in this scope. It is also assumed that when military leaders rise to these ranks and appointments, the majority would have exhibited the basic leadership attributes of character, courage (both physical and moral), competence, commitment and compassion. In my understanding and experience, the key roles and imperatives of strategic leadership are detailed below.

A Vibrant Politico-Military Interface

- It is important for strategic military leaders to comprehend the existing and emerging politico-economic-social milieu and relate it to the strategic scenario, as it may unfold under different circumstances. Strategic military leaders would often be called upon to make strategic decisions as part of a collaborative process, and therefore need a very clear understanding of how the government functions and does its business based on "Allocation of Business Rules (AOB)" and "Transaction of Business Rules (TOB)".[5] The unfortunate truth is that most military leaders grapple with these issues only on reaching exalted positions, to the great disadvantage of the organisation. Apart from short tenures, inadequacy of "Professional Military Education (PME)" leaves most unprepared to function at the strategic level.

- In a thriving democracy like India, civilian control by elected representatives of the people is an absolute imperative. However, that's not how it has translated on the ground, with the politician disinclined and the bureaucrats enjoying power without responsibility and accountability. Moreover, the armed forces are mostly not major influencers at the policy formulation stage, though are required to execute such strategic policies. The forward defence policy adopted in 1962 against professional military advice led to catastrophic outcomes. The seven decades of relationship between the civil and the military had the doyen of strategic thinkers in India, Mr. K. Subrahmanyam, call it the "Absent dialogue".[6]
- When senior military leaders formulate military strategy and operational plans, these must be based on political-strategic guidance; in the absence of an articulated national security strategy, one is not sure of this maxim's veracity in our context. It is therefore incumbent on strategic military leaders to advise and guide the political decision makers on such critical aspects to avoid catastrophic mismatch during crisis. This can only happen when such military leaders fully comprehend the Clausewitzian maxim that war is a continuation of politics with other means.

Visionary and Transformational Leadership

- There is general unanimity that strategic leaders need to be Visionary and Transformational. The words of Rev. Theodore Martin Hesburg, President of the University of Notre Dame for 35 years (1952-1987) are very pertinent, "The very essence of leadership is that you have to have vision. You can't blow an uncertain trumpet." This applies across the board and is especially true of Strategic Military leaders.
- Vision in simple terms means an ability to see into the future, an ability to imagine, how things or ideas could shape up, even when they do not exist physically as yet. Such an ability has to be of course based on deep study and experience, as also on deeply embedded beliefs and a highly developed sense of intuition. Visionary leaders are those who are able to capture the futuristic and potential needs of their organisation and are also able to move their organisation in a direction that realises those needs in the best possible way.

- However, strategic military leaders are not hoisted at the top, but have been filtered up, after serving in the organisation for many decades, hence they are already party to and well versed with the organisational vision. As Lt Gen Anit Chait explained at the CDM seminar on visionary leadership in 2013:[7] "in the armed forces when people reach the top, they do not have to bring in a completely new vision, but only a distinct flavor, as part of their personality imprint on that vision, so that it remains dynamic to the emerging and envisaged challenges and organisational needs." Continuity with change may be a good description.
- When you look at the Indian Armed Forces, Gen K. Sundarji stands out for his visionary outlook. On assuming the appointment of COAS in 1986, he conceptualised a vision document 2020, that envisaged a generational change from the conventional attrition oriented, to a modern high-technology warfare.
- The traditional model of leadership has been transactional in nature, seeking to achieve an outcome through an exchange of value(s). Transformational leadership on the other hand seeks to go further, satisfying and responding to higher missions and purposes, harmonising the individual and the organisation, changing the status quo in the process.[8]
- There are four factors that comprise transformational leadership: idealised influence, inspirational motivation, intellectual stimulation and individual consideration, all combining to create performances that exceed organisational expectations.[9] Transformational leadership focuses on team building and motivation to push for higher performance levels, by creating an environment where individual genius can flourish leading to collective growth of the organisation.
- Can Transformational Leadership flourish in the armed forces? The answer is a definitive "Yes", but for this to happen, you need to create an enabling environment. It would be fair to say that Visionary and Transformational leadership would go hand in hand in the armed forces.

Preparing for the Role

No one is a born strategic military leader, nor does tactical brilliance prepare you to be one. The job requirements are different; as the saying goes, a "General is not a superior Colonel", though it's axiomatic, we often find comfort in doing the subordinate's job. The organisation has to recognise and prepare you to be one, through right grooming, exposure and enhancing the PME, as distinct from training. Pitchforking an unprepared General to the top slot, without the benefit of the above, is being unfair both to the individual, as also to the organisation.

- Two contrasting cases come easily to mind, General Eisenhower and Field Marshal Sam Manekshaw, the former without war experience prior to World War II, the latter a War Veteran. What is common amongst the two is their wide exposure, PME and grooming through key appointments. In current times, a look at the qualifications of US Army General David Petraeus would be quite revealing. Apart from his brilliant service record and exposure, he earned a PhD degree in international relations in 1987 from the Woodrow Wilson School at Princeton University and also undertook a fellowship at Georgetown University. These foundations were to hold him in good stead, when he took up strategic military leadership positions in the Middle East.
- A strategic leader needs to be wearing reading glasses and simultaneously have a 20-20 vision for the future. For the micro perspective he has staff, subordinates and assistance of technology, but outlining, understanding and propagating the macro picture is clearly his domain. A quote by Abba Eban, an Israeli diplomat, captures this dilemma very well: "A senior leader who keeps his ear permanently glued to the ground, will have neither elegance of posture, nor flexibility of movement."

At Ease in a "VUCA" (Volatile, Uncertain, Complex, Ambiguous) Environment

- At the lower tactical level, you deal with black and white, but as you rise up the ladder, specially at the operational and strategic level, shades of grey creep in. If you have not prepared yourself to be at ease in a "VUCA" environment, you will get stumped. There has to be high tolerance for ambiguity with an ability to take decisions with 60-70 per cent of desired inputs. This comes with the development of "Military Intuition", a combination of your PME and experience. Unfortunately, our ethos prepares us to be at ease in a black and white environment, most ill-suited for tackling the challenges of the 21st century. This has to change.

- A strategic leader should have a high quotient for risk-taking and optimising the opportunities that arise. He should be able to discern wheat from chaff and put his finger on the "Schwerpunkt" (Point of Main Effort), from amongst the vast information and propositions that are available to him. It is axiomatic that if strategic leaders keep in a conference all day, they will never hear the silent knock of opportunities.

Creating an Enabling Environment

- Creation of an enabling environment where the subordinates can hope to achieve their genius is the hallmark of a strategic leader. Harmonising and aligning the individual aspirations to the organisational goals should be the desired result. That is the only way to leave a lasting legacy and secure the future of the organisation.
- Genuine and constructive professional dissent needs to be encouraged in the armed forces, specially at the senior level, since its exclusion would only encourage mediocrity and predictability. Let's also be clear that, "Blind conformation is not loyalty, nor independent thinking dissent."[10] There is also a larger context in which to understand strategic military leadership; it is harmonising of external influences on the internal thinking and strategies, especially the politico and economic considerations. Therefore, a strategic and visionary military leader doesn't operate only from within, he stands at the margins of the internal and external environment, and without compromising on the core values, optimises the best outcomes for his organisation.
- Visionary leaders should not be afraid to challenge the status quo culture and embrace change, even though it may result in short-term turbulence. They must stay the course and not be dissuaded by short-sighted vested interests. The challenge is all the greater, where results may not be visible in your tenure, but will certainly benefit the organisation in the long-term.

Authority-Responsibility-Accountability

- Authority-Responsibility-Accountability is a key essence of military leadership, specially at the senior levels; in fact, this is what distinguishes the armed forces from various organisations on the civil side, where this linkage is rarely, if ever, established.

- The Indian armed forces are good at establishing personal accountability, but fall short as far as professional accountability is concerned; Kargil is a good example. It is believed that the Army's Kargil after action report was contested in the Armed Forces Tribunal and Supreme Court, who ruled against any changes.[11] Questions have also been raised regarding the levels at which accountability was established, post Kargil. One is also not aware if any accountability has been established post Uri, Pulwama and even the recent Chinese intrusions in Ladakh, including the loss of precious lives at Galwan (Ladakh).
- The US Army lost its moorings after WWII, when they stopped establishing operational accountability, leading to Vietnam. Thomas Rick covers it in great detail in his book, *The Generals*, which should be recommended reading for all operational and strategic military leaders. Questions on accountability have also been raised recently, after the unprofessional exit of the US Armed Forces from Kabul, and that too from within the organisation. Sharing credit and taking the blame is a linked attribute desirable in operational and strategic military leaders. It is essential that such leaders develop "broad shoulders and large heart", along with an ability to enforce strict action when necessary, in the interest of the organisation.
- Apart from ensuring this linkage in subordinates, a great responsibility also rests with the apex level military leadership, to ensure that the armed forces are prepared and provided the minimum, if not optimum wherewithal, to be able to carry out their role and operational responsibilities effectively. It reflects poorly that every time there is a crisis, there is urgent activity for emergent purchases of arms and munitions. Many examples come to mind; shortage of critical ammunition for tanks, and of course the depleted number of fighter squadrons for the Indian Air Force. This has obviously not happened overnight and everyone understands the time required to recoup these assets. This reflects poorly not only on the Government, but more so on the top hierarchy of the armed forces, and is a matter of serious strategic and intellectual concern.

Reinforcing the Core Values

- The core values, which define the essence of the Indian Armed forces, which also provide the foundation on which the armed forces function, may be under stretch in the 21st century. Of the core values the one causing maximum concern is the "Apolitical Nature" of the Armed Forces. Let's examine this in some detail.

- The armed forces as an institution do not have any political preference, they serve the constitution of the country and take legitimate orders from the government of the day. In the past there have been some incidents which cast a shadow on particular senior officers crossing the line, but these have been few and far between. Of late, the political climate has raised concerns that we may be entering a grey zone, either unknowingly or with the acceptance of a few in key positions.
- National security has become a major issue in the electoral battle, with ownership being established by political parties, also encompassing the armed forces. This has been further exacerbated by polarisation amongst the veterans, of the kind not seen before. Whilst it is legitimate for veterans to engage in political activity, they have to be mindful that their activities/ views do not spill over into the serving lot.
- The above notwithstanding, the armed forces remain true to the core values, though they have to be mindful of the challenges they may face in future. In this, the strategic military leadership has to play a crucial role in ensuring that the "Apolitical Nature" of the armed forces is zealously guarded and reinforced.
- The senior veterans also have an onerous duty to ensure that their conduct in politics remains in harmony with the dignity of the uniform they once wore. A responsibility also rests with the political class to not transgress on the apolitical nature of the armed forces.

Speaking Truth to Power

- At the level of strategic military leaders, they need to virtually discard the words, "yes, sir" from their lexicon. In the interest of national security, they must stand up and convey the harsh truth to not only the military hierarchy, but also to the political authority, however unpalatable it may be; for, any dilution in the facts may cost the nation dear. Yes, there will be pressure to conform, but this is where leaders of mettle need to stand up to their convictions. The title of this book aptly describes this onerous responsibility: *Men of Steel #Military Leadership for India.*

- The example of then Chief, Gen Manekshaw, illustrates this best, when he advised the prime minister to defer operations against East Pakistan from pre- to post-monsoon and in the winter months. It is to the credit of both that this advice was accepted, leading to a resounding victory in December 1971.
- Recently, when President Trump of USA declared that the US was ready to strike 50 cultural sites in Iran, this was openly contradicted by Joint Chiefs of Staff Chairman, General Mark Milley, who clarified, "we will follow the laws of armed conflict".[12] On another occasion he reiterated "the Armed Forces of USA take an oath to the constitution of the country—not to any king, queen or any individual, a country, religion or tribe".[13] It was a crystal clear message to the political establishment, not to politicise the US Military.

Victorious Will and Calmness in Crisis

A victorious will is a quintessential imperative for a successful strategic leader, it is also infectious. Many examples abound in military history; closer home, then Lt Gen Manekshaw, when he arrived in NEFA to take charge after the 1962 debacle, issued his famous statement, "Gentlemen I have arrived, there will be no withdrawal without my orders and those orders shall never be issued." Similarly, when it seemed India was facing a great disaster at Khem Karan in the 1965 Indo-Pak conflict, it was the calmness displayed by Western Army Commander, Lt Gen Harbaksh Singh that saved the day, and Pakistan's offensive was routed at Asal Uttar soon thereafter.

Ethical Responsibilities

- Being the last resort of the nation and dealing with life-and-death issues, the whole edifice of the armed forces is based on trust and ownership. Therefore, strategic military leaders have to constantly uphold ethics and probity and reinforce trust and ownership. It has to be a "top down, top first" approach, there is no other way.
- Having tenanted key operational and strategic appointments, I can summarise this by stating: "What some leaders did, that shouldn't have been done; and what some didn't do, that they should have done."

- It is certainly challenging to be good, when all around you standards of ethics and probity are falling. For the armed forces there is no other choice, and the senior hierarchy has to show the way.

Conclusion

The critical role strategic and operational level military leaders play in a nation's destiny has not received due recognition in India. Such leaders are required to not only have a good understanding of the politico-strategic environment, but also provide vision and direction to the instrument of last resort, to ensure the security and well-being of the nation.

Strategic military leaders also have the onerous responsibility to harmonise the external influences with the internal strategies, and without compromising on the core values, obtain the best outcome. Drawing strength from the constitution, when most others may be hesitant, the strategic military leader has to be able to speak the truth to power, for anything short of it, may have serious consequences for the nation.

Within the organisation itself, strategic military leaders have to define/reinforce the long-term vision and create an enabling environment, based on trust and ownership, where professionalism and merit can flourish, leading to optimum effectiveness and battleworthiness of the armed forces. For these roles, both the individual and the armed forces have to prepare the leaders to shoulder such onerous responsibilities.

"Whether a man is burdened by power or enjoys it, whether he is trapped by responsibility or made free by it; whether he is moved by other people and outer forces or moves them—this is the essence of Leadership."

—Theodore H White

Notes

1. *ASCI Journal of Management*, September 1, 2014, based on a lecture delivered by Lt Gen AK Singh, on June 11, 2014.
2. JS Bajwa, "Defining Elements of Comprehensive National Power", *CLAWS Journal* (India), Summer 2008.
3. Lt Gen AK Singh and Lt Gen Raj Shukla, "Changing Nature of the Conflict in 21st Century", Chapter 3 of the book, *Military Strategy for India in the 21st Century* (New Delhi: KW Publishers, 2019).

4. Ibid.
5. CDM Secunderabad, Annual Seminar on Visionary Leadership, November 22-23, 2013.
6. Rakesh Sharma, "Civil-Military Dynamic: Making of Military Strategy", Chapter 14 of the book, *Military Strategy for India in the 21st Century* (New Delhi: KW Publishers, 2019).
7. n. 5.
8. CDM Secunderabad, Panel discussion on "Transformational leadership in changing times", 2010.
9. Transformational leadership, IAFS Extension, University of Florida, powered by EDIS.
10. AK Singh and VK Ahluwalia, "Military Leadership in the 21st Century", Chapter 17 of the book, *Military Strategy for India in the 21st Century* (New Delhi: KW Publishers, 2019).
11. *Indian Express*, August 24, 2019.
12. CNBC, January 7, 2020, Natasha Turak.
13. Gen Mark Milley, Speaking at Fort Belvoir, Virginia, November 11, 2020.

2

Preparing Operational Leaders for Conflict in the 21st Century

BS Dhanoa

Introduction

India's armed forces have delivered in wars of the last century, in no small measure due to the excellent level of tactical leadership provided by direct leaders in the Army, Navy and the Air Force. Equally, in most conflicts, higher-level leaders stepped up to the plate when needed and broke down political imperatives of going to war into achievable operational and tactical level objectives. The Armed Forces have had their share of failures and setbacks as well, 1962 and the intervention in Sri Lanka in 1987 come to mind when reflecting upon poor politico-military decisions made by a hierarchy not well skilled in thinking through second order effects, and military leaders not being straightforward in pointing out pitfalls to political superiors, when asked to undertake operationally challenging or unviable tasks. Between India's last major military operation, Op Vijay (Kargil 1999) and recent standoffs in Sikkim and Ladakh, one could make a bold statement to say that the very character of warfare in these 20 odd years has undergone a change. No longer are militaries likely to witness long periods of mobilisation of forces, a preparatory period of build up and then a clear-cut campaign against a known adversary (or adversaries). There is a greater likelihood of sudden flare-ups in critical areas, which have the potential to snowball into larger conflagrations if not responded to speedily, and all against a backdrop of outwardly normal relations with the adversary in other domains. Such warfare challenges the very notion of standard doctrinal response options and conventional preparedness levels, so well known to the armed forces. It needs a certain kind of military leader who is comfortable in operating outside the established boundaries of war and conflict. It calls for well schooled and experienced military leadership at all levels, especially at the operational, which is the most challenging and difficult level, for it is here that campaigns are planned in detail and executed, forces directed and decisions that affect the very survival and wellbeing of tactical units pitched into the direct fight, made and reviewed.

Military Leadership in the 21st Century

The basic framework of leadership needed for leading men in uniform hasn't really changed much since warfare underwent a transformation, starting with the Napoleonic Wars in the early 19th century, the coming of the industrial age of warfare with the two World Wars and the dropping of the atomic bomb, while closer home the Indian military paved the way for the existence of Bangladesh. Whereas the tools for waging war have changed tremendously, and still continue to do so at a rapid pace, some tenets of leadership remain as solid as foundational blocks for military leaders. These are character, courage (physical and moral), conduct, intellect, care for the men and women under a leader's charge, sound military knowledge, physical endurance, and mental stability to withstand the stresses and strains of modern warfare. Whether you are a direct, or an organisational and/or strategic leader, these leadership traits are needed, in varying proportions, to prepare and sustain a military for the challenges it faces. It may also be germane to the discussion to bring in the levels of warfare, as are commonly known, i.e., the tactical, operational and strategic, to try and understand the requirements placed on military leaders as they climb the hierarchical ladder in service. Some would prefer to directly equate the levels of warfare with levels of leadership. So, as per this school of thought, command up to a certain size of fighting units or formations (battalion, brigade, division, etc.) across the three services (even though it is a force fit at times for the navy and the air force) is by tactical leaders, above that till field armies or equivalent is considered operational, and top leaders, who conduct and orchestrate military strategy for the nation as a whole and are the interface with the political representatives of a country, count as strategic leaders. It is felt that today such clear boundaries between levels of leadership and warfare are really not possible given the speed and span of communications, the different means available to nations to wage war, and the effects of small actions by tactical leaders that potentially have ramifications at the operational and strategic levels. The most recent example being the clash at Galwan in June 2020, between Indian and Chinese troops, which set in motion a politico-strategic rift that is yet to be resolved, with serious implications for the diplomatic and economic ties of both nations. Therefore, as this piece looks at the needs of leadership in the 21st century for Indian military leaders, there is a definite coalescing of the levels of warfare. Operational leaders, especially, who are the focus here, need to possess a mental make-up and attitude that allows them to operate across all levels. This, clearly, will place greater demands on them physically and intellectually and thus the preparation and education of such leaders must commence early.

Professional Military Education and Operational Leaders

Professional Military Education (PME) occupies a reasonable space today in the honing of key leadership traits and staff skills of military officers that are essential for any modern military to operate at peak efficiency and be effective in a crisis. From joint services training academies, to staff and war colleges the aim is to impart service specific and joint training to tactical leaders that enhances the war waging capability of fighting units, while operational leaders and staff officers function to keep plans, intelligence, information operations, logistics and civil military relations balanced, and the national effort focused. It is unfortunate that in our context, an extended commitment in counter-insurgency (CI) and counter-terror operations has given us a generation of officers primed for such operational planning and conduct, but who are mostly unfamiliar with the greater rigours and complexities of planning for conventional conflict with a peer adversary. This is an issue that even the US military, the most committed operationally for many decades, has had to deal with as it pulls out of Afghanistan and reorients efforts to take on threats from China and Russia.

There is also a definite need to have a set of military officers who are well grounded in theories of joint warfare, military strategy and leadership, operational art, geography and history, weapons development, operations and tactics, as also international relations, economics and geopolitics. They are the key functionaries at strategic and operational levels who will convert political directives to the armed forces into discrete military objectives, recommend/assign forces best suited to achieving these, and ensure their adequate equipping and preparations in peacetime to meet expected, and unexpected, requirements. A hazy grasp of what the operational level is all about due to a small operations' mindset that comes from excessive CI exposure will also have to be reoriented within the PME syllabus. This is no easy task and currently the methodology is to select and impart education in this broad sweep of subjects to a small cohort of officers, who have been determined to possess the potential to rise in their careers (a very subjective assessment), and assign them to attend courses at war colleges/defence universities at home and abroad.

The Future of War

If there is one thing that history teaches us, it is that whatever may be the preparations for future war, militaries are invariably trained and equipped for the last war. It is only those nations, whose military leaders are mentally agile and able to modify doctrines and plans as the new situation dictates that will probably emerge victorious. Even the luxury of time to understand and assimilate how an adversary is posing new threats may not be available to operational level commanders in the future. They would have to rely on their critical thinking skills and levels of flexibility inbuilt in fighting forces' doctrines and tactics to overcome such challenges on the battlefield, without losing cohesion and unity. Thus to have such capabilities within a military, or more specifically a joint field fighting force, leaders at all levels of command have to change the way they train and educate themselves and their subordinate military commanders, to face the realities of a future conflict that no one can predict with any certainty right now. This is when we have not even factored in major challenges of how to deal with the introduction of artificial intelligence driven decision cycles, information overload due to the ever increasing numbers of opto-electronic platforms that are gathering terabytes of digital data about potential threats, and the introduction of 'game changing' new weapons systems that can take decisions and act autonomously, all overshadowed by the ever-growing threat of cyber and nuclear doomsday.

Honing Future Operational Commanders

As can be analysed from some of the issues that future operational commanders are expected to deal with, their basic training and education in the arcane arts of the fighting forces, as also higher-level preparations to deal with unforeseen threats, has to be visionary and detailed. A cursory look at various militaries' steep learning curve since early 2020, which the onset of the SARS Cov-2 Pandemic has forced them to adopt in all spheres of military preparedness and assistance, is a good example of the need for such agility and readiness to deal with unexpected threats. Therefore, for future operational commanders, a set of regular and 'out of the box' recommendations is offered herein:

(a) First and foremost, change the paradigm of selection of operational level leaders from the tactical sub-set that we currently follow. Identify and mentor (as a formal process) those who show early signs of being able to see the 'larger picture' and have the ability to plan for contingencies and effects that most may not visualise. At which point in service should such identification and selection be done; that is a key issue. This inflection point may arrive at varying stages across the three services. However, for future joint occupation of billets in operational headquarters, it is recommended that the staff college could be the start point for such selection and formal mentoring. The current fixation with command and staff billets for all officers who pass staff college needs to be shed. Once officers are put through their paces in staff college, the possibility of another year of military education for identified officers (via a voluntary written exam) could be considered. They would go on to be operational planning staff and would occupy key billets across the spectrum of military functions in joint HQ. This idea is not something new but is akin to the establishment of the School of Advanced Military Studies (SAMS) that the US and other NATO allies did back in the 1980s, and which paid dividends in both Iraq wars in the planning and execution of complex military operations.

(b) Second, allow select officers, as they transit through their mid-level careers, the freedom to take a year or two off (yes, the much maligned and revamped study leave) to research and do their PhD in a set of subjects taught in universities with excellent faculty for strategic studies, national security and other associated fields that today are essential to deal with an interconnected world. This must be done prior to inducting them into high pressure and key posts in active areas. The whole career management chart by the personnel branches of the three services must undergo a radical change to allow 'educated mavericks' to also exist and flourish along with regular gladiators. Not easy to do, but it is an idea whose time is here.

(c) Third, officers must go purple (i.e., joint) in the envisaged theatre commands at the first opportunity and serve outside the narrow confines of their individual services and parochial patronages, which only allow for a certain kind of individual to succeed in the pyramidal structure of military ranks. Even the bifurcation into command and staff (originally envisaged by General Sundarji) for those best suited for plans and those for field forces needs to be relooked and brought into vogue so as to have a well skilled general staff that can advise and draw up detailed contingency plans without having to re-invent the wheel. This is again anathema to the conventional mindset and will have to be force fitted into the personnel department plans for selecting future operational leaders.

(d) Fourth, the way in which services, singly and jointly, exercise and train for possible future scenarios must be revamped completely. The need to assess the potential of future commanders based on such training events has to be done away with and we must be honest in all training activities, to seek and to find those individuals that display originality (very difficult in current circumstances), are not afraid to experiment and lose in training simulations as long as the intent is right and have the courage to speak their minds when asked for solutions to military problems. Right now the whole set-up is skewed towards a single thought process that mirrors the thinking of the leaders at the apex of the operational hierarchy. It is once again a huge hurdle to be overcome. But if this is not done, then for every success in battle, there would be an equal number (if not more) of failures. Officers have to be encouraged to be forthright, open in their communication with seniors and subordinates and to have the courage of conviction to stand their ground if the situation affecting an operational outcome so demands. This is key to building genuine professionals in the unforgiving business of planning for victory.

(e) Fifth, we must make use of opportunities provided by bi- and multi-lateral cooperation with other militaries to actually position operational staff in HQ with foreign forces and let them be contributors and learn from their counterparts. Current small exercises with foreign forces are inadequate to impart the right lessons and inputs needed for future combined and joint operations. We do imbibe a bit of such training with UN forces but that is a peculiar sub-set of military peace operations and not enough billets are ever available to train a larger set of officers. Our desire to be indigenous and self-reliant in our military thinking goes counter to such global military best practices. It must not become a virtual millstone around the necks of operational leaders in the future. If another nation or military does it better, let's learn from them by sending our officers there. So, in short we need to overcome hesitancy to interact and absorb from our foreign counterparts, and the internecine wars between the MEA and MoD over military cooperation and diplomacy should be discarded for larger common national goals.

(f) Lastly, there is a crying need to broaden the executive decision-making perspective of operational level military leaders by their experiencing the sinews of governance at national and international levels. This is a field very few are exposed to because of the way our 'steel frame' of governance is set up. The military remains apolitical and outside of the politico-diplomatic and economic domains that dictate national security policy. By the time they are expected to provide answers to challenges that the political leadership may face, they are incapable of a cogent institutional response as very few (if any) have had exposure to the 'system' earlier in their careers. To offset this, spending a couple of years on deputation to key ministries, within the country and even abroad, is recommended for identified military officers. Such cross-pollination of minds has been a recommendation of many committees on national security and defence, most notably the Kargil Review Committee. It is widely resisted by the civil servants but it is an idea whose time is long overdue.

Conclusion

The need to have articulate, mentally agile, well-educated and critical thinking operational leaders is an established one. No military can do without the crucial middle rung of staff and operational commanders who have to work in conjunction with strategic brass to translate hazy political and strategic guidance into clearly defined military lines of operation. They need to draw up instructions for the joint force, provide the necessary wherewithal to complete the envisaged mission, and lead the joint force till the successful execution of given tasks. India's armed forces are going to face a myriad of challenges in the conventional and the sub-conventional domains in the period ahead, with known adversaries already knocking at the doors, posing threats anew. Military commanders at strategic and operational levels would be expected to provide 'professional advice to and execute plans of' the political and civilian hierarchy, to meet such challenges. The recommendations mentioned herein, specifically for improving the capabilities at the operational level, are but the tip of the proverbial iceberg. Better ideas can definitely be thought of and put in place gradually, to ensure that in the 21st century India's Armed Forces are well equipped intellectually and temporally to meet a rising nation's demands.

Major General **BS Dhanoa** (Retd), was commissioned into the Armoured Corps in December 1983. He last served in the Army's premier institution, the Army War College, where his primary role was the mentoring and education of future military leaders of the Armed Forces. He has also commanded an armoured brigade and an infantry division on the Western Borders. His passion is to write and speak on Military Leadership, Operational Art and the Future of Conflict.

3

Shortfall in Senior Leadership

1962 and 1965

Shiv Kunal Verma

The seeds of the military disaster in 1962 were sown almost a decade before the actual fighting erupted in both NEFA and Ladakh on October 20, 1962. In January 1949, the Government of India, then barely a year-and-a-half in office, had given a clear and subtle message that at the end of the day, the prime minister and his close circle of advisors would call the shots in a military conflict. The decision not to press home the advantage from Uri towards Dommel and Muzaffarabad defied military logic, especially since the tribal *lashkars* and the Pakistani Army had pretty much shot their bolt. With Prime Minister Jawaharlal Nehru choosing to follow the Governor General Louis Mountbatten's advice to refer the matter to the UN instead, there really was no organised set-up within the service headquarters or the Defence Ministry then under Sardar Baldev Singh who could vociferously oppose or question the decision.

Nehru's various comments about India not needing an Army in the years that followed the ceasefire have to be taken with a pinch of salt, for when it came to it, India did not exactly shy away from exercising the military option. In October 1947, the Junagadh landings cut off the princely state from Pakistan, after which the military again came into play in September 1948 in Hyderabad against the *razakars* and the Nizam's state forces. In 1956 the Naga National Council declared its intent to secede from India, which again resulted in the deployment of the army (and, to a limited extent, the

IAF) within the country, which then culminated with Op Vijay in Goa in December 1961. With the army, air force and the navy all getting into the act versus the Portuguese, no wonder then that President John F. Kennedy wryly remarked that Nehru's armed intervention in Goa was akin to "finding a priest in a whorehouse".

In all the above operations, the tactical handling of the situation was left to senior officers in Army Headquarters. The Indian Army, which had built for itself a formidable reputation during World War II, was not tested in any of these operations, other than perhaps the insurgency in Nagaland which at the time was a different kind of a challenge, and the aura of India's Armed Forces remained intact in the eyes of the general public. From all accounts, the army was a good place to be in the 1950s, with some of India's finest getting commissioned as institutions like the Joint Services Wing (JSW)—which was the forebear of the National Defence Academy at Khadakwasla—the Indian Military Academy and the air force and naval acadamies coming into their own. Life was as much about training as it was about Dinner Nights and Blue Patrols, traditions that had been left behind by the British.

The problem, however, was not with the junior leadership. Most officers who found themselves elevated to senior levels at the time, seem to have been out of their depth. Most had been fast-tracked into ranks they were actually not prepared for, and since a majority of them at the time were either KCIOs or ICOs, they seem to have operated in an orbit that was quite removed from the reality of geopolitics and the changing scenario all around them. There were exceptions—people like General Thimayya, Lt General SPP Thorat, Brigadiers P Bhagat and DK Palit—whom one can classify as "thinking officers", but the majority seemed quite content to be in their cocoons.

In 1949 when Mao Zedong's communists overthrew the Kuomintang and formed the People's Republic of China, it did not impact India in any way as at the time China was a far-off entity, with Peking nowhere on New Delhi's radar. But then things were destined to move at a breath-taking pace—with Mao first establishing Chinese control over Sinkiang and then marching into Lhasa to claim Tibet in October 1950. For India, it was crunch time, but the army chief at the time, General (later Field Marshal) KM Cariappa, virtually refusing to entertain any thought of military intervention. In an emergency meeting, the Director of the Intelligence Bureau, BN Mullik, was told by Cariappa that if

India was to intervene in Tibet, all that could be spared was a single infantry battalion!

Sardar Patel's letter dated November 7, 1950 to Prime Minister Nehru in which he warned of Communist China's expansionist mindset, preceded the Home Minister's demise by a few days. However, perhaps as a result of the points raised in the letter, Nehru set up two committees that were asked to submit their report on the new 4,000-km long Indo-China frontier that had suddenly come into being. Both the reports were remarkable—the Lt General Kulwant Singh report warned the government that there would be a border clash with China in the next decade, while the Major General Himmatsinghji report on the North and North East Border Defence Committee virtually provided the blueprint for the physical occupation of the McMahon Line. These two reports, combined with Exercise Lal Qila that was conducted in March 1961 in Lucknow by Thorat which was an appreciation of Chinese intent, shows that there were enough people in Army Headquarters who were professionally competent, but then almost all of them were either superseded or brushed aside sooner or later.

The rapid rise of Lt General BM "Bijji" Kaul and the role played by the Defence Minister, Krishna Menon, were two key factors that would impact the performance of the Indian Army in 1962. While the former made his way up the hierarchy despite negative reports because he had Nehru's hand on his head, Menon's style of functioning resulted in not just the humiliation of Thimayya, but also the side-lining of Thorat. More than the personalities involved at the time, it is perhaps more pertinent for us to actually focus on the rejection of what was being advocated in Lal Qila per se.

In Exercise Lal Qila, Thorat had pointed out that a Chinese attack in and around October/November 1962 was but a foregone conclusion. He had then spelt out his plan which was to firm up on a Defensive Line where the logistical advantage would be with India. The Assam Rifles, at that point, was holding the posts on the actual crest lines and Thorat proposed they would fall back in a systematic manner and harass the advancing Chinese by threatening their communication and supply lines (they had performed a similar task during WWII when they functioned as Victor Force behind the advancing Japanese lines). The rest of the army, properly dug in and fortified, would then take on the PLA. This line that was to stretch across the entire length of NEFA

(Arunachal), would extend from the Mandela Heights and Bomdila in the west to Hayuliang in the east.

The Thorat Plan was junked to a man by the pro-Bijji Kaul lobby for by then it was obvious to most which way the sun was rising. To fight on the crest line was, from a military point of view, sheer madness. But by then the Forward Policy had come into vogue and with Kaul as the QMG, precious resources were used in both Ladakh and NEFA to move and supply troops in places like DBO, Galwan, Hot Springs in the west and various posts in the east. By the time the Chinese did come calling at Dhola in September 1962, the fact of the matter is, the Indian high command had no clear-cut plan of action to counter the threat. Ad hoc and knee-jerk reactions once the balloon goes up, can only create chaos, and that is exactly what happened across the board in 1962. Neither the chief, General Pran Thapar, nor the Eastern Army Commander, Lt Gen LP "Bogey" Sen, had any previous experience of the Tawang Sector. On October 10, when Kaul (by then designated the IV Corps Commander) rushed to Delhi and told Nehru the Indians were in no position to fight on the Nam Ka Chu, both these officers chose to oppose Kaul and insist 7 Brigade put up a fight if indeed the Chinese attacked from their current vulnerable position.

7 Brigade's collapse after 2 Rajput positions on the Nam Ka Chu were overrun was actually unexplainable. Both the commanding officers of 9 Punjab and 4 Grenadiers abandoned their positions, and with their units in tow, made good their escape, in the process even abandoning their own men who had to fend for themselves. Brigadier John Dalvi, whose brigade HQ was overrun, was trying to get to Hathung La when he was captured. After the screen positions at Khenzemane were overrun, the divisional HQ at Zimithang was also abandoned. The helicopter allotted to the GOC 4 Mountain Division having also come a cropper, Major General Niranjan Prasad then had to make it back to Tawang where he arrived when the Battle for Bum La was raging.

The hurried exit from Tawang and the subsequent ad hoc fortification of Se La, was followed by a 24-day break in the fighting. Prasad was removed from command, but his replacement, Maj General Pathania, did little to inspire confidence by setting up his divisional headquarters at Dirang Dzong, almost 70 km from Se La where four infantry battalions were deployed. On November 17 when the Chinese resumed their advance, apart from a brief instance where 4 Garhwal Rifles was dug in, the Indian performance was a disaster. Poor tactics, no understanding of the terrain, and the complete absence of higher leadership led to a disaster which for any army is hard to live down. Thembang, Bomdi La, and even Wallong to the east, saw platoons and companies left to their own devices. Individual battalions fought—4 Garhwal Rifles at Nuranang, 6 Kumaon at Wallong and 13 Kumaon at Rezang La in Ladakh, but it was a case of too little, too late. In each of these cases, whatever success these units had, the senior commanders failed to build on their performances. Almost all the Indian casualties would take place during the disorganised fall back.

India's humiliation was complete with the hasty and completely unwarranted abandonment of Tezpur and the North Bank in Assam. Unaware of the impending ceasefire (the Indian embassy in Peking deciding to send the declaration in "code" to New Delhi), the COAS, General Pran Thapar resigned while Prime Minister Nehru abandoned any hope of covering himself even with a fig leaf by prostrating himself before Kennedy, literally begging the United States to send its air force to come fight India's war. One of the greatest ironies until that moment was the refusal of the Indian leadership to use the IAF in an offensive role, but that then is quite another sorry and tragic story!

With the Chinese declaring a unilateral ceasefire, the Indians got a breather and time to regroup. In any other country, there would have been questions asked and answers sought, and those found wanting would have been shown the door, at the very least. As far as Mao was concerned, having achieved his stated aim of clipping Nehru's wings, the Chinese leader could sit back and watch the Indian prime minister try and recover his equilibrium. Nehru then made two critical appointments, both of which were surprising under the circumstances. Yashwantrao Chavan, the sitting chief minister of Maharashtra was appointed the defence minister while Lieutenant General "Mucho" Chaudhuri was appointed the army chief (without being elevated to the rank of a General).

Chavan made no bones about the fact that his main priority was to protect the prime minister from being blamed. In the process, he also took the decision that no civil bureaucrat or army officer would be brought under the scanner for his performance. The Henderson Brooks Report was a classic case in point as was the hushing up of officers who were subsequently repatriated from China in May 1963. Dalvi's book, *Himalayan Blunder: The Curtain Raiser to the Sino-Indian War of 1962*, though self-exonerating in nature, was initially banned, until Upendra Arora of Natraj Publishers, Dehradun, finally published it in 1969. As a result of this, almost every officer who abandoned his post or failed to do his duty even in Army Headquarters or elsewhere, simply carried on as if nothing had happened.

Ever since the Chinese debacle in 1962 and the near complete collapse of India's leadership—both civil and the military—there was an air of inevitability about a war between India and Pakistan. With the British still refusing to accept that they were the "'has-beens' in the new world order", their colonial hangover meant they were even more obsessed with Kashmir than any ordinary Pakistani citizen, who like the majority of his Indian counterparts, was probably more concerned with just staying alive and feeding his family. With the bloodbath of Partition and the first round of fighting over Kashmir still fresh in most minds, a tottering India was too much of a juicy target for a cocky Pakistan that was bursting at the seams with state-of-the-art weaponry.

The US and British aid that came in post the 1962 debacle had the string of Kashmir attached to it. To complicate matters even more, Lord Louis Mountbatten was in and out of India, pushing Nehru into not only releasing Sheikh Abdullah but also filling the airwaves with optimistic talk about finding a Kashmir solution. With Nehru's passing away on May 27, 1964, the elevation of Lal Bahadur Shastri (mainly to keep Morarji Desai at bay) to the post of prime minister melted whatever reservations President Ayub Khan may have had about an armed settlement. The worst part of unending propaganda is that sooner or later you start believing it yourself.

For Pakistan to militarily impact India and force the incomplete agenda of Partition vis-à-vis Kashmir, its armed forces had to do an encore of 1962. That Pakistan viewed the Indians as being *buzdil* (cowardly) and incapable of standing up to them had a lot to do with the stance taken by the then foreign minister, Zulfikar Ali Bhutto, who in the pre-DNA era had convinced a fair majority of Pakistanis that they were descendants of Islamic marauders who had repeatedly plundered the subcontinent. President Field Marshal Ayub Khan, who had not particularly distinguished himself in combat during WWII, seemed more hesitant to commit Pakistan to war, being far more focused on creating military alliances and economic development. However, especially after Ayub let Bhutto rig the Presidential election in his favour, the enigmatic and belligerent foreign minister, egged on as he was by Mao Zedong himself, was hard to rein in.

On the Indian side of the border, General Chaudhuri was an enigma. Even "Mucho" the writer, who spouted wisdom in Indian newspaper columns on military matters, probably would have been hard pressed to pass judgement on the Indian army chief. There can be no doubt about the man's personal bravery as a young officer, for he had eight Mention in Despatches, which must be a record by itself! Thrust into the limelight first during Op Polo in Hyderabad and then again in Op Vijay in Goa, he seemed more intent in cornering personal glory than anything else. The plan he had worked out for the liberation of Goa using 1 Armoured Division would have ensured the Indian army never reached Panaji even if the Portuguese had got up and gone home. Fortunately for him, at the time he was the acting chief (General Thapar was away in England) and he was giving orders to himself as the Southern Army commander, and his grandiose but completely impractical plan had been shot down by both CGS and the DMO.

Two years later, Chaudhuri was the man at the helm, fate having handed him a basket full of silver spoons! Having seen favourites like Thapar and Lieutenant General Bijji Kaul abruptly crash to the floor from their carefully polished pedestals, Chaudhuri would prove to be an astonishingly cautious general, refusing to rock the boat in NEFA even after the Chinese withdrew, even ensuring the army did not reoccupy its own land!

With Chavan making sure no one was brought to book, and once Chaudhuri had ensured his *bête noire* Kaul went home in disgrace, the army chief and his style of functioning made him the single point man in the government's dealing with the armed forces. With an 11-year age difference between the army chief and the CAS, Air Marshal (later Hon Air Chief Marshal) Arjan Singh, the avuncular relationship reduced the IAF to a subordinate position. Vice Admiral (later Hon Admiral) Bhaskar Sadashiv Soman, the CNS was even younger to the air chief. But not that it mattered, for the navy was not on Chaudhuri's decision-making radar altogether.

The IAF on its part, whenever it was called in, delivered with telling effect. However, just what were General Chaudhuri, Lieutenant Generals Harbaksh Singh (Western Army Commander) and Jogi Dhillon (GOC 11 Corps) thinking during their multiple meetings during Op Ablaze in the build-up to the fighting in September 1965, is a mystery. Dhillon on his part was one of the few who had escaped getting the axe in 1962 because as officiating CGS he had repeatedly blundered.

As luck would have it, we do know that Major General Niranjan Prasad, who was removed from command for "cowardice" in 1962 but had since been reinstated, had ironically repeatedly asked for air cover during the wargaming, but had been ignored completely. When the advance on Lahore along the Grand Trunk Road on September 6 floundered due to communication breakdowns and repeated air strikes by the PAF, neither the army commander nor the corps commander ventured beyond 15 Divisional HQ just west of Atari. Yet, despite almost all accounts by junior officers talking of the destruction wreaked from the air, Harbaksh Singh in his post-war writings dismissed the effect of air attacks as being negligible. This simple fact was subsequently accepted by almost all commentators as the gospel truth! Covering up blunders, unfortunately, seems to be the norm.

Lt Gen Harbaksh Singh on his part, as the army commander, was as guilty as Chaudhuri, and keeping the IAF out of the equation during the early part of the war would cost India dearly time and again. Arjan Singh, who also attended at least one of these conferences, also seemed reluctant to plan for the use of the IAF in an aggressive manner. In 1991 when I met him in connection with my film on the history of the IAF, *Salt of the Earth*, he clearly recalled that it was only after the PAF attacked our airfields and there were civilian casualties when they hit the Amritsar Railway Station and the Jodhpur Jail, "were the gloves off!" Air Marshal Bharat Kumar in his documentation of IAF history says the restriction imposed by the government was in relation to striking at Pakistani bases and had not been communicated down the chain of command by the CAS, leading to a lot of frustration when pilots were just sitting around. Be that is as it may, just because the GoI had laid down that no pre-emptive strikes could be launched, keeping the air force out was inexcusable.

There were of course certain unavoidable restrictions. The UN mandate that no fighter aircraft could be based in the Valley needed the army to think minus offensive air support, but then the same also applied to the PAF. General Chaudhuri was in Srinagar on September 1 when news of Op Grand Slam reached him. Despite repeated reports of the Pakistani build-up, both the corps commander, Lieutenant General Kashmir Katoch and the army chief had decided in their heads there was no chance of a Pakistani attack along that axis and had even refused to issue anti-tank mines and had in fact, pulled out 2 Sikh from the sector. When the "balloon went up", in a bizarre turn of events, Chaudhuri departed from Srinagar at 1000 hours and instead of going to New Delhi (a DC-3 Dakota would take three hours plus) he instructed the pilots to take him to Pathankot instead. In the hour and a half he spent at the air force base, the Vampires were told by the station commander to be prepared to go to Chhamb in support of the ground troops.

If we follow the timeline on that day, Chaudhuri reached Chavan's office at 1600 hours, spoke briefly to Arjan Singh in the defence minister's outer room, and then the two chiefs met Chavan who agreed to clear the air strikes. Arjan Singh had pointed out the danger of collateral damage since there were no clear bomb lines, no previous knowledge of the terrain, and no Forward Air Controllers who could guide the aircraft. The choosing of Vampires as the leading three formations has since led to many a heated debate, but what actually transpired at Pathankot between 1100 hours and 1300 hours shall never really be known. In later years, Arjan Singh was too much of a gentleman to not take the responsibility for what subsequently happened, but the fact remains the air strikes, even though quite a few accidentally hit Indian positions, halted the Pakistan advance by at least 48 hours.

It is perhaps easy to be critical with hindsight of how things unfolded 59 and 56 years ago, but there is no getting away from the fact that the Indian chief had violated just about every basic tenet of warfare. He not only split the forces into two different sectors—Lahore and Sialkot—he also left himself vulnerable to a Pakistani thrust that seemed to obsess his thinking as the fighting escalated when there was just a thin green line being held by a handful of battalions of 4 Mountain Division at Asal Uttar. Choosing to fight a battle of attrition against an enemy whose entire defensive line was stretched out along the Ichhogil Canal, Chaudhuri literally threw in the towel by advising Shastri to accept the ceasefire when he should have been pleading for another five-six days to do what a general is supposed to do—annihilate the enemy and destroy his war making ability!

The commanders invariably are the ones under scrutiny for, at the end of the day, the buck stops with each man at the top. The loneliness of command, where every decision can cost lives of men, is a thousand times amplified in combat. Harbaksh Singh is perhaps a classic case where his unbridled aggression deflated Op Gibraltar—by going for Haji Pir when his immediate subordinate commander was more inclined to fight the raiders in a conventional manner, or his refusal to fall back on the Beas River when the two men above and below him had gone into a panic. But, then, he was the same man who failed the troops on the ground by sticking to his own assessment when things went horribly wrong, as was the case in Khem Karan after the armoured threat had been neutralised. The obvious differences between him and Chaudhuri eventually hurt the Indian side a lot more.

The 1962 clash and the 1965 War are both stories of tremendous courage displayed by young officers and the troops as men fought tenaciously whenever they were called on to do so. There were moments of extreme courage and sacrifice, of cowardice, of men dying and men who were let down by their commanders. If anything, this has perhaps been India's greatest failing, for we seem almost determined to shy away from the truth. The government of the day would rather gloss over events rather than worry about future generations drawing the right lessons from any clash. Unless we as a country develop the culture of shifting the chaff from the wheat, we will always sing ballads for some who are undeserving, and glorify others who actually need to be brought to book. That is perhaps the only way to get past the Greek scholar Aeschylus's famous words, "In war, truth is the first casualty."

Shiv Kunal Verma was educated at the Doon School and Madras Christian College. He then worked with *Tiger Tops* in Ladakh reconnoitering trekking routes in the early 1980s. After journalistic stints with *India Today* and the *Associated Press,* he shot and directed the Project Tiger television series for *Sanctuary Films* in the mid 1980s. Under the banner of *Kaleido India,* he went on to shoot and direct numerous films that involved working extensively with the Air Force, Navy and the Army. He is also the author of several books including *Ocean to Sky: India from the Air; The Long Road to Siachen; The Northeast Trilogy; The Assam Rifles; 1962: The War That Wasn't* and *1965: A Western Sunrise.*

4

Redemption: The Revival of Strategic Leadership in 1971

Arjun Subramaniam

Backdrop

The 1960s were a roller-coaster experience for India's fledgling strategic leadership. After the morass of the 1962 politico-military bungling that led to a humiliating military defeat at the hands of the People's Republic of China, there was only one way and that was up. However, the absence of political stability following Nehru's death in 1964, left national security in the lurch in the hands of a well-meaning and politically experienced Lal Bahadur Shastri, who assumed the mantle of prime minister following Nehru's death. While Shastri did his best to revive the Indian military's broken morale and restore its dented leadership by appointing the hardy Maratha politician, Y.B. Chavan, as the defence minister, the 1965 conflict with Pakistan was merely a small step in the revival of confidence within the country that India's political leadership and armed forces were capable of defending India's security interests. The death of PM Shastri at Tashkent in early 1966 resulted in political chaos and it was the unlikely figure of India's first woman prime minister, Indira Gandhi, who succeeded him, to steer a remarkable transformation of strategic leadership from the time she assumed office.

Early Revival

It is a fallacy to believe that the revival of strategic leadership began only in the run-up to the 1971 war; it began in 1967 on an altogether different front, the China front. The Nathu La skirmish in September 1967 resulted in hundreds of casualties suffered by both India and China, however, India stood up to Chinese aggression and responded to fire with fire. Rather than displaying traditional Indian diffidence vis-à-vis China, PM Indira Gandhi backed the military leadership in Eastern Army Command through the skirmish and stayed calm through the crisis. Interestingly, the three army generals who were in the thick of action, Lt Gen Manekshaw, the Eastern Army Commander, Lt Gen Jagjit Singh Aurora, the GOC of 33 Corps and Maj Gen Sagat Singh, the GOC of 17 Mountain Division, would find themselves in East Pakistan four years later, orchestrating the collapse of the Pakistan Army.

Storm Clouds Gather

As the crisis in East Pakistan imploded into a spiralling security challenge for India as millions of refugees streamed into India following a military crackdown orchestrated by the Pakistan Army, PM Indira Gandhi made a decisive choice as early as March 1971 to use force to compel Pakistan to cease its aggression against the Bengalis of East Pakistan. A key departure from earlier times was the clarity with which Mrs. Gandhi made up her mind to use force to further India's strategic objectives. This resulted in even the normally accurate and conservative CIA to overestimate her war objectives. In a secret memo issued on December 7, 1971 it listed out her war objectives as "liberation of Bangladesh, the incorporation into India of the southern area of Azad (Pakistan-held) Kashmir and the destruction of Pakistan's armoured and air force strength so that Pakistan can never again threaten India."[1]

Indira Gandhi even queried her Army Chief, General Manekshaw in April 1971 whether it was possible to launch an attack into East Pakistan immediately. This she did after being thoroughly and rightly briefed by India's intelligence agencies that the humanitarian crisis had the potential to assume humungous proportions in the months ahead. She is reported to have been a trifle disappointed that Manekshaw had a watertight case for asking for time till December to build-up his forces, rather than rush headlong into conflict weeks before the onset of the monsoon. Complementing the army chief's cautious view by advising restraint till all diplomatic options were exhausted was Indira Gandhi's affable Foreign Minister, Swaran Singh.[2] That Indira Gandhi listened to them was indeed quite creditable considering that she was quite a dominating personality. The lessons of 1962 and 1965 loomed on the horizon as Manekshaw wanted to have his forces better-trained, better-equipped and ready for battle.

Supporting Manekshaw in a remarkable show of solidarity, Admiral Nanda, the naval chief, and Air Chief Marshal Lal, the air chief went about readying their forces for battle with remarkable vigour and professionalism. Some military analysts and historians feel that Manekshaw was excessively cautious and influenced heavily by the fear of failure. As a result, they say, India missed a golden opportunity to stop the un-calibrated massacres in East Pakistan, as also stem the flow of refugees into India. Others like John Gill, a South Asia expert at the National Defence University, Washington, and the author of a definitive monograph on the war, add that Manekshaw was waiting for the winter so that any kind of Chinese intervention could be ruled out.[3] Manekshaw's scepticism of the Chinese was understandable for he had been given the unenviable responsibility of commanding the Indian Army's Eastern Army Command in the years following the 1962 debacle. He had done a great deal to restore the fighting spirit and élan of the units in his command and had no intention of frittering away those gains.

From July to November of 1971, Indira Gandhi and her Foreign Minister, the affable Sikh, Sardar Swaran Singh, assisted by a few other astute negotiators globe-trotted across the Western world, attempting to build a consensus to force a UN resolution condemning the Pakistani atrocities in Bangladesh. Realising that Nixon's planned historic visit to China in 1972 would have a negative impact on Indo-US relations despite Kissinger's assertions to the contrary, India wasted no time in sealing a Friendship Treaty with the Soviet Union in August 1971.[4] The treaty effectively paved the way for accelerated Soviet military assistance and diplomatic support in the build-up to the conflict. There was no procrastination in seeking Soviet help as India realised that any UN resolution on East Pakistan would be vetoed by both the US and China and that it was important to solicit Soviet help to block any kind of international censure should India get embroiled in any conflict with Pakistan. After a successful visit to the Soviet Union in September, Prime Minister Gandhi failed to make any headway in her talks with President Nixon on the last lap of her visit to the West in early November. She returned to India knowing that India had no option but to go to war. It is only after her return that the Indian

Army commenced its full-fledged probing attacks into East Pakistan along with the Mukti Bahini.

The Players

The larger than life personalities of Indira Gandhi and General Manekshaw (later Field Marshal) have dominated the strategic discourse of the 1971 war. Not having commanded forces in battle in the 1947-1948 conflict with Pakistan as many of his contemporaries did, and missing the action in 1962 because of falling out of favour with the Defence Minister and the army chief, Manekshaw had a point to prove. With his flagging career having been resuscitated after the 1962 debacle, he was given command of Eastern Army Command in 1964 to repair the damage done after the Chinese stormed into NEFA. Little did he realise that fate would keep him out of action in the 1965 war too as India did not open a second front in the east except for brief battles in the air. It is in such circumstances that when presented with an opportunity to do battle, he was determined to make it count!

Sharing centre stage with them was the earthy Jagjivan Ram, a shrewd political associate of Indira Gandhi's who replaced Y.B. Chavan as the Defence Minister in 1970. With his predecessor having done all the hard work in rebuilding India's armed forces and somewhat restoring its pride and élan, Jagjivan Ram delegated complete responsibility to the service chiefs and established a close personal relationship with each one of them. By doing so, he won their respect for his astute and "hands off style of functioning". He was the quiet orchestrator of 1971.

Like Manekshaw, Pratap Chandra Lal had gone through a rocky decade prior to being appointed as the Air Chief. A victim of Defence Minister Krishna Menon's high-handedness, Lal's services were terminated in September 1962 over a disagreement with Menon on replacements for the ageing Dakota aircraft while on deputation to the Indian Airlines Corporation. Luckily for Lal, he was reinstated in December 1962 after Krishna Menon fell from grace in the wake of the 1962 debacle. After highly successful stints as Air Officer Maintenance, Vice Chief of Air Staff during the 1965 War and Chairman of Hindustan Aeronautics Limited, he took over as Chief of Air Staff in July 1969. By then this intellectual and "thinking airman" had acquired a comprehensive view of what needed to be done to ensure that the IAF emerged as an equally important element of joint operations. He was the transformational leader the IAF was looking for.

The Indian Navy was seething after it was kept out of action during the 1965 war for no fault of its own making, and like many senior naval officers, Admiral Nanda, the Chief of Naval Staff (CNS) was determined to make amends for the "no-show" in 1965. Baptised into the navy during WWII and having seen the famous "revolt" of 1946 as a young officer, he gained vital operational experience on India's first warship, INS *Delhi.* Nanda's major contribution was in convincing the political establishment that maritime power would have a major role to play if India wanted to establish clear military supremacy over Pakistan. He, more than anyone else, infused the self-belief in the Indian Navy and propagated an offensive mindset amongst his operational planners.[5] His insistence on creating a reasonably potent Eastern Fleet and unleashing the INS *Vikrant* on Chittagong, Cox's Bazar and Khulna ports despite the submarine threat from the Pakistan Navy was one of the defining moments of the war.

Though intelligence gathering in the western sector remained as scanty as it was in 1965, significant credit for the success of covert operations in Bangladesh must go to R.N. Kao, the chief of R&AW, the hush-hush outfit that was hived out of the Intelligence Bureau (IB) in 1968 specifically for the conduct of covert operations. A close confidant of Indira Gandhi, the flamboyant Kao came into his own during the period of April-December 1971 as he orchestrated a psychological warfare campaign in East Pakistan and set the ball rolling for the training of the Mukti Bahini by the Indian Army in camps which were set up secretly in the eastern parts of India. His role has to be seen in the light of Indira Gandhi's desire to commence the Bangladesh campaign in April 1971. When Manekshaw was candid enough to indicate that he was not ready, Kao stepped in to keep the East Pakistan pot boiling till the army chief was fully prepared.[6]

Two distinguished civil servants merit special attention for their enabling role as effective and approachable interfaces between the military and the political establishment. They were Mr. P.N. Haksar, the Principal Private Secretary to the PM and Mr. D.P. Dhar, who headed the Foreign Policy Planning Committee in the run-up to the conflict. These two kept the service chiefs continuously updated on diplomatic parleys and political discussions through the Chairman of the Chiefs of Staff Committee—it was teamwork of the highest order and very rarely was it to be repeated during future contingencies.

Decisive Outcomes

India emerged as the clear regional power in South Asia after the 1971 war with Pakistan by demonstrating significant national will to tackle a crisis of enormous proportions. A concurrently well executed politico-diplomatic-military strategy with clear objectives for much of 1971 allowed India to explore all possible options before resorting to military action in East Pakistan. By diplomatically engaging with Russia, Western Europe and the US, and sensitising them about the ongoing human tragedy in East Pakistan and the spiralling refugee crisis in India, the Indian government succeeded in conveying to the world that it wanted a peaceful solution to the problem. However, the speed with which it commenced military operations indicated its resolve and willingness to use military force in pursuit of its national interests.

Clear and congruent strategic objectives from both the PM and the Defence Minister, along with effective politico-military interfaces between the service chiefs and key interlocutors from the Prime Minister's office resulted in a commonality of purpose. Capability building was given top priority and the service chiefs enjoyed a fair degree of independence when it came to designing their concept of operations. Even though the Indian Army and its talismanic chief Manekshaw retained their importance as "first among equals" in a predominantly land-centric armed forces, Indira Gandhi and Jagjivan Ram, her portly and jovial Defence Minister, realised the value of air and maritime power in a two-front battle. Due credit must go to them, Air Chief Marshal PC Lal and Admiral SM Nanda for transforming Indian air and sea power from being mere adjuncts of land power, into tools of military power that had the ability to contribute significantly to a joint military campaign. This ensured that Manekshaw as Chairman of the Chiefs of Staff Committee had no other choice but to create joint-warfighting capability by amalgamating air and sea power into his overall theatre battle plans in both the eastern and western sectors.

There is little doubt that the metamorphosis and "hardening" of Indian diplomacy took place in the run-up to the 1971 conflict. As the crisis unfolded and the India-Pakistan war ended in a decisive victory for India, both Nixon and Kissinger were clearly irked by Indira Gandhi's assertiveness and refusal to cower before US hegemony in the region. Her refusal to get rattled by the posturing of the Seventh Fleet, only increased their frustration at not being able to coerce India into ceasing military operations before its objectives were met. Hard-ball realpolitik coupled with a fair degree of empathy for the suffering population of East Pakistan forced Indira Gandhi to "do the right thing" and wage what can easily be called today as a "just war".

Notes

1. "CIA Memorandum", December 7, 1971, declassified June 2005, US State Department Documents pertaining to India and Pakistan 1971, p. 219. Assembled by Ramesh Shanker, at http://www.indianmilitaryhistory.org/
2. J.N. Dixit, *India-Pakistan in War and Peace* (New Delhi: Books Today, 2002), pp. 182-83.
3. John. H. Gill, *An Atlas of the 1971 India-Pakistan War: The Creation of Bangladesh* (Washington: NDU Press, 2003), p. 13.
4. For an excellent commentary on the treaty four decades after it was signed, see Arun Mohanty, "Toasting the Legacy of 1971 Indo-Soviet friendship Treaty", August 9, 2011, at http://in.rbth.com/articles/2011/08/09/toasting_legacy_of_1971_indo-soviet_friendship_treaty_12842.html. Accessed on March 7, 2015.
5. From a book review of Admiral Nanda's book, *The Man who Bombed Karachi,* by Ashok Mehta at http://indiatoday.intoday.in/story/book-review-of-s-m-nandas-the-man-who-bombed-karachi-a-memoir/1/204795.html. Accessed on February 10, 2014.
6. For a detailed review of R&AW operations in Bangladesh and the legacy left behind by its founding Director, see B. Raman, *The Kaoboys of R&AW: Down Memory Lane* (New Delhi: Lancer, 2007), pp. 9-14.

Air Vice Marshal (Dr.) **Arjun Subramaniam** AVSM (Retd), is the President's Chair of Excellence in National Security Affairs at National Defence College, New Delhi. He is an accomplished military historian and the author of *India's Wars: A Military History 1947-1971* and *Full Spectrum: India's Wars: 1972-2020.*

5

The Kargil War

A Story of Grit, Determination

Mohinder Puri

Introduction

The Kargil War in 1999, without a doubt was thrust upon us by a perfidious enemy by encroaching into large areas across the Line of Control (LoC) in the Dras-Mushkoh and Kargil-Batalik Sectors and the country was taken by total surprise. The visit of our Prime Minister to Lahore in February 1999 and signing of the Lahore Declaration created a sense of complacency and consequently a dropping of guard, leading to declaration of near war and an unprecedented loss of lives. While we repeatedly fail to learn from history, nevertheless, a number of issues need to be flagged to ensure that the lives of our bravehearts were not lost in vain.

This war has been a subject of a plethora of case studies and articles and the causes and fallouts discussed threadbare in various fora. However, as General Officer Commanding (GoC) of India's premium Mountain Division during that period and the fact that I saw and participated in the battles from a unique position, study of the battles, its causes and lessons learnt, from my perspective, should, hopefully offer a better insight. I have covered this article in two parts, as under

(a) Part I. Critical Analysis and lessons learnt

(b) Part II. Hope of success vs Fear of failure: Dilemma of contact military leadership.

Part I. Critical Analysis and Lessons Learnt

Poor Intelligence with Zero Accountability: It has been repeated, ad nauseam, that one of the main causes of our national embarrassment was the failure of intelligence. Although, information was fed to both the civil and military intelligence agencies, they failed to interpret the information and convert it into actionable intelligence. We had no idea of the build-up of infantry, artillery and logistics in the Northern Areas of Gilgistan, during the previous campaigning season and were taken by surprise on discovering the establishment of numerous posts by the Pak Army over a frontage of approximately 130 km. It is quite apparent that Pak used the latter part of the winter season to intrude in strength across the LoC by exploiting the large gaps in our defences, including those winter vacated posts vacated by us by mutual understanding. Evidently, the troops in contact failed to carry out winter patrolling or surveillance as per laid down instructions and standing operating procedures. While the lack of intelligence was a major failure, what was equally intriguing was that no one was made accountable for this lapse. One would have expected stringent action against those responsible, but to the best of my knowledge that was not to be. *Failures due to lack of professionalism must not be ignored and must be dealt with fairness and firmness.*

Again, on accountability, you would recall that the Group of Ministers chaired by Mr. LK Advani had recommended that manning of the border should be with the BSF or ITBP wherever required. Since the responsibility to maintain the territorial integrity lies with the Army, manning the borders by different organisations operating under the control of a different Ministry leads to contradictions. *If the paramilitary organisations need to man the border, they must be placed under the operational and administrative control of the Army, both in peace and war.* War and security are serious business and should not get buried in turf war between ministries.

While on the issue of accountability, I must narrate an incident which merits some consideration. One of the battalions in North Kashmir was not performing up to the mark, and on an occasion, an IED blast was set off by the terrorists on the brigade commanders' vehicle approximately 200 yards from the battalion HQ, during a routine visit of the commander to the unit. Fortunately, the commander escaped with minor injuries. Evidently, the battalion was underperforming and this incident reinforced my views. Later, on outbreak of hostilities in Kargil, since the battalion was one of the early ones to be inducted from the Valley, it was tasked to act as a reserve in the first main operation of the division, on an objective which had defied capture for three weeks, and on its completion capture the next feature on the ridgeline. They were required to speedily build up and be prepared for their given task. However, during my visit to the brigade HQ, I found the commanding officer at his battalion base while the battalion had concentrated for its reserve task. He indicated to me that he was physically not in a state to move up to the battalion and he would conduct the operations from the base. I immediately relieved him of his command and since the second in command was empanelled for Lt Col, I asked him to take over command and informed the Corps Commander of the developments. The change in command at a critical juncture had an impact on the battalion and besides capturing their objective, they performed exceptionally well in subsequent operations, finally winning two of the highest gallantry awards and the title of "Bravest of the Brave". *Good leadership can have an inspirational effect on a unit as proved in this case.*

What was also very glaring that, except for a couple of commanding officers along with a brigade commander who were held responsible, no one in the higher ranks was made accountable for their performance leading up to the events of the Kargil war.

Performance of Various Levels of Leadership: Along with the issue of accountability, is the performance of various levels of leadership. Without exception, the young officers including sub-unit commanders, performed bravely, courageously and at times beyond the call of military duty. We lost many young officers leading from the front and all of them left a mark of their commitment and involvement in achieving their assigned tasks. To them must go a great deal of credit for our victory. However, the performance of junior commissioned officers (JCO) left much to be desired. Besides the age factor, domestic responsibilities inhibited them from taking bold risks and leading by example. I feel a separate study would be in order to analyse whether we do require this rank in the present-day environment. The commanding officers, except for a handful, successfully led their battalions and regiments, and overcame stiff enemy opposition despite heavy casualties. Their involvement with their command, despite their age, was commendable and they shared the difficulties and privations with their men. The ones who didn't perform well, were suitably dealt with during and after the war. We seem to have reduced the age profile of the commanding officers and this is a welcome step. The brigade commanders too were in the higher age bracket but to their credit they were not restricted by this and performed commendably. Again, *those who underperformed were appropriately dealt with by the system.*

Zero Error Syndrome: We have often spoken about working in a "zero error syndrome" and how it impacts on the environment's work culture. Some of the units on induction in mid-May 1999 were given tasks for which they were neither acclimatised nor properly equipped to undertake operations in extreme high-altitude terrain, with the result they were unable to accomplish their tasks and had incurred heavy casualties. However, for no fault of theirs, they did not earn a good name and were blamed for having failed in achieving their task. A unit lives to ensure that its name and glorious traditions are not tarnished. Since wars do not take place every day, it may take a unit years to redeem its reputation as and when a future conflict takes place. I was sensitive to this issue and despite odds gave the concerned units a second chance. It was gratifying to note that all of them performed to their peak and earned many awards including the Unit Citations and "Bravest of the Brave". I am also of the view that units which do not perform well are not entirely to be blamed and their failure must be shared by the immediate superiors in the chain of command. *Units must be launched into an operation with complete readiness and confidence that they would return victorious.*

Higher Leadership: On higher leadership in the military, the selection for higher command is indeed of great importance and though our selection system has stood the test of time, it needs to be given a relook to ensure that the best talent is approved and fielded into battle as and when the occasion arises. Even in a no-war situation, *good leadership is of essence for keeping the military machinery well-oiled and ready to take on any task.* Now that we have a Chief of Defence Staff (CDS), and the Theatre Commands are very much on the cards, the selection process of ranks two stars and above needs to be given a fresh look. I would suggest that the Selection Board be held under the aegis of the Raksha Mantri with the CDS and the three Chiefs as members and the Defence Secretary as the secretary of the Board. This process will thus have a tri-service character and hopefully the right talent will be spotted for the selection of Theatre Commanders, the Chiefs and CDS.

Style of Leadership: Coming to the style of leadership or attributes of a good leader, we all have our own characteristics, but there are certain issues which need to be kept in mind, more during war than in peace. From my own experience, I feel that consultative leadership is important during evolution of your plans, and all stakeholders must be taken on board to formulate a workable plan which has a high percentage of success. While the final decision lies with you, discussions with your staff and commanders goes a long way in accomplishing a task successfully. Subordinates look up to commanders who are accessible and communicative and those who will hold your hand when the going gets tough. *It is good to remember that the credit for all successes must go to your subordinates, and omissions and commissions must rest squarely on your shoulders.*

Handling Pressure: War confronts you with many challenges and handling pressure is one of the more predominant factors which can impact the minds of commanders and consequently influence the course of events. The type of pressure a commander is subjected to also depends on the level at which he is operating. The bottom line is that we all face pressure in some form or the other either from the superior headquarters or from the environment including the media or from within our own organisation. While I did not face any pressure from any of the higher headquarters except on an odd occasion on some minor issue, which is understandable, I did feel the pressure of the enormity of the task and the deadlines which I had set for myself. However, I ensured that in my capacity, I kept the environment free from all the pressures and allowed the subordinate commanders to execute approved plans with boldness and without fear of consequences. We must *train our commanders that when under pressure they must have shoulders broad enough to absorb the pressure and not disseminate it to their subordinates*, as any attempt to pass it down, is a sure recipe for disaster.

Nature of Future Wars: A word on the nature of future wars and the threats to our national security. I am of the view that threats from our two neighbours will be confined to disputed areas and a conflict escalating to the western plains sector is unlikely for various reasons including crossing the nuclear threshold. The centre of gravity has to shift to the mountains and our organisational and equipment profile must keep this in mind. However, this is not to say that the plains sector should be neglected in terms of resources. While we shift our focus of war preparation to the disputed areas, we must retain a strong deterrence in the plains sector. Coupled with this are the new technologies which are likely to be fielded, like cyber-attacks, unmanned aerial vehicles, drones, artificial intelligence, and so on which are in the process of being operationalised in most modern armies including the People's Liberation Army (PLA) of China. While boots on the ground will remain predominant, the employment of technology as a force multiplier should be factored into our plans. This will also entail a *reorientation in our training methods for which the Schools of Instruction must be geared up to meet the challenges.* I am sanguine that action would be in hand to look into these aspects.

Role of Media: Lastly, it will not be out of place to mention the role of the media, which undoubtedly is a force multiplier. In Kargil, the media was highly successful in bringing the war into the drawing rooms of the nation. The inhospitable terrain with all its difficulties, hardships in fighting in extreme high-altitude area, and experiences of young officers after every operation were some of the visuals which identified the public with the Army. The electronic and print media were full of stories of the heroism of the troops, with the families of the martyred soldiers proudly claiming sacrifices of their kin. However, in the early stages there were stories in the print media which were factually incorrect and had a negative impact on the image of the army and the units being launched into battle. The initial policy was flawed and when some freelancers printed their stories, the army banned the media in the war zone. But soon better sense prevailed and a media policy was formulated which by and large met our requirements. *The army and the media both need to understand their strengths and lay down a code of conduct in war which ensures transparency to the extent that it does not jeopardise own operations.*

Conclusion

Generals are often blamed for fighting the last war. I do hope our present and future military leadership disproves this hypothesis and concentrates on the basics to ensure that when war does break out, they are up to the expectations of the country and bring victory and glory to the nation.

Part II. Hope of Success vs Fear of Failure: Dilemma of Contact Military Leadership

Introduction

Hope and Fear are two predominant emotions of our daily life. Hope is an optimistic state of mind based on expectations of positive consequences in relation to some forthcoming venture, decision or planned or unplanned event in our day-to-day functioning. Fear, on the other hand, brings a set of unpleasant emotions which manifest in the mind in the form of danger, pain, failure, fear for one's loved one's personal safety, and besides, in the military the fear of damaging one's organisation's honour and dignity. In this article, I will attempt, through my personal experience, to translate the emotions of "Hope of Success" and "Fear of Failure" on the minds of military commanders at all levels who are engaged in the combat zone with the enemy. At the back of one's mind, these two emotions play a major role in influencing one's decision-making.

8 Mountain (Mtn) Division (Div), which I had the honour to command, was deployed in the counter-insurgency grid in North Kashmir and was located at Sharifabad, on the Srinagar bypass to Gulmarg. By mid-May it became apparent that the Pakistan Army's intrusion was, inter alia, aimed at internationalising the J&K problem and changing the alignment of the LoC. It was also obvious to a military mind that existing resources of 3 Infantry (Inf) Div were inadequate to meet the challenge. I, consequently, suggested to the Corps Commander to induct my Div to augment the resources and divide the area of responsibility between the two Div's. While the Corps commander also had similar thoughts, it was after considerable deliberations at the Corps, Command and Army Headquarters that the decision to induct 8 Mtn Div into battle was taken. Commanders in the chain are frequently confronted with situations which require a choice between equally undesirable alternatives. Both the alternatives, that is to induct my Div for restoring the situation, or maintain status quo and plan for an additional formation from outside the Command Zone for the task were viable alternatives. While inducting the Div across Zoji La gave an advantage of availability of additional troops, the impact of this action would cause a vacuum in the counter-insurgency grid and leave the area for exploitation by the militants. However, both the options

carried a hope of success and a fear of failure, adding to the uncertainty of decision-making. It is thus essential that contingency planning is put in place to cover the apprehensions of failure. Consequently, when my Div moved out for operations, appropriate adjustments in the counter-insurgency grid were made to overcome the vacuum created by denuding the grid. A Rashtriya Rifles (RR) Sector (Div size) was raised in North Kashmir and the RR Heaquarters moved to Srinagar from Delhi.

I assumed operational responsibility of the Dras-Mushkoh sector on June 1, 1999. The first view of the terrain as one crosses Zoji La is awesome and one is struck by the high mountain peaks varying in height from 18,000 ft to 21,000 ft with valleys at 10,000 ft to 11,000 ft above sea level. The situation in the Dras-Mushkoh sectors was tense and since mid-May we had not met with any success. Casualties were mounting and there was a discernible impression that the enemy was having the better of us. The fog of war was taking a heavy toll on troops who were fighting in the most inhospitable terrains with shortage of weapons and equipment. In the midst of this demoralising environment, the task of commanders becomes that much more difficult and challenging. *In such an environment, and in an atmosphere which is filled with despondency, where the morale of the rank and file is at its lowest, where no success has been met despite efforts made in this direction, and where there is very little hope for the situation turning for the better, the leaders have an onerous and an unenvious task. In this state of uncertainty, hope and fear are more or less juxtaposed in the mind, and are in constant conflict, adding to the dilemma in the process of decision-making.* I must confess that seeing the enormity of the task, I too had many a time apprehensions for the success of my Div, which occasionally impacted the analysis of the task at hand.

The above notwithstanding and despite setbacks on the battlefield, **leaders cannot sit back and put themselves and their command in a state of inertia.** The situation called for a speedy response since we had a small window available to restore the sanctity of the LoC before the onset of winter and closure of Zoji La. Keeping my hopes and fears aside, I concentrated on galvanising resources for the first attack on a feature which had defied capture for three weeks and was the deepest intrusion across the LoC making movement on the highway restricted to hours of darkness. I took twelve days to build up the battalions, artillery and logistics to ensure that when we launch the first attack, it should be executed with full preparation with all contingencies covered. *Confidence* *in your command and ecosystem give you enough strength to see the brighter side of the outcome and to an extent put your fears to rest. You take a decision with the confidence and hope of its success and though you may have passing waves of fear, these get overtaken by your preparedness for the task.* The attack was launched with complete preparedness and with the ardent hope that it would succeed and give us the first glimmer of hope for the next phase of the battle. However, all plans do not follow the path chalked out by you and the best of plans can go awry for a variety of reasons. At first light I was informed that the enemy was still holding out and further progress during the day was not tactically feasible. Although this news was shattering, I told the commanding officer to firm in and make an attempt to overcome the remnants on the objective at an opportune time. While contemplating the future course of action, a lot of negative thoughts passed through my mind, and I must confess, the fear of failure was perhaps the most predominant. Again, *you can't sit back and let events overtake your thinking faculties.* It is important to sit down calmly and plan a course of action which would give impetus to the existing situation as well as clarity for planning the operations. Fortunately, within a short time I was informed that the commanding officer of the battalion had seen a window of opportunity and in a bold manoeuvre launched a platoon against the enemy holding out on the objective. Imagine the battalion commander's dilemma at this crucial stage of the battle. If he had waited for last light, his task would have become that much more difficult as the enemy would have reinforced the position; and if he took action during broad daylight, he carried the fear of incurring casualties. *Whenever in doubt, it is better to take control of your fears and opt for the bolder course of action.* The battalion commander did exactly that, and succeeded in capturing the remaining objective with minimum damage but with a lesson worth retaining.

In war, since there are no prizes for runners-up, all commanders are focused on attaining their assigned tasks with success. The path to this success is paved with a number of ups and downs, hopes and fears. While "hope" carries with it a sense of optimism, "fear of failure" on the other hand can cause the mind to be immobilised and cause the mental faculties to stop rationally thinking of the future course of action. Every plan evolved on the battlefield carries a percentage of failure. Whether this percentage is high or low depends on the commander's state of mind. Since time is at a premium, particularly when in contact with the enemy, **quick decision-making** is essential and commanders must **address alternatives** to reduce or minimise the chances of failure. Thoughts of failure must be considered as transitory and at no stage should they cloud a commander's mind and deny him the ability to speedily and correctly take decisions. This situation is very likely and probable at the battalion and lower levels. **While higher commanders have the luxury of more time to formulate decisions with more inputs and alternatives, the commanders at the lower level have restricted availability of time to respond to dynamic battlefield situations.** As I have mentioned above, the prompt action taken by the battalion commander at a critical juncture of the battle changed the course of the war and turned the tide in our favour. Success to a large extent relies on your ability to leverage failure and the taste of our first success paved the way for our subsequent operations. This objective which brought us our first victory had earlier defied capture, and for three weeks the battalion tasked to capture it, was not meeting with success. The battalion had established a firm base and had reached a stage of inactivity except for an odd ill-planned operation which cost them some casualties. A mental block had set in and this immobility in planning for a fresh initiative was very apparent. A sense of failure had overtaken the commanders. However, the same battalion after a minor success in a supportive operation, developed a sense of confidence and positivity resulting in the capture of the most dominating height in the sector and earning for themselves a number of well-deserved awards. It is this same battalion in which a young soldier dared the enemy and even after receiving seven bullets into his body, managed to inflict a number of casualties and assisted his sub-unit to overcome the opposition. He was awarded the country's highest gallantry award. An analysis after the operation on the thin line dividing bravery and cowardice; or hope and fear was informally done in my interaction with a few of the living awardees, and **it transpired that though fear of failure or their own survival did cross their mind, the adrenalin which was pumping into their system, overcame their apprehensions and gave them the strength and hope of dutifully accomplishing their task.** *The stronger and overriding emotion was for preserving their and their unit's "izzat", "naam" and "nishan".*

In a warlike situation, every plan for an operation carries the risk of failure and **while evolving the plan, commanders must take cognisance of the chance of failure which can result despite best efforts in its execution.** While the brilliance of your plan may carry the hopes of success, it is that odd chance of its failure and the risk in execution that you fear the most. To overcome this state of mind, **multiple contingency plans** are made, their number dependent on the level at which the operation is being planned. **These contingencies must cater for maximum viable eventualities, and need to be backed by good planning with allocation of adequate resources. Therefore,** *when you launch troops into battle, the chances of success must far outweigh the fears of a failure.*

Conclusion

It therefore transpires that the two emotions, hope and fear, greatly influence the minds of those engaged in close contact with the enemy. As to how these emotions pan out is really dependent on the leaders and individuals. In my experience, I have observed that **commanders who evolve plans and execute them in the spirit of hope, optimism and positivity, have a better chance of success in battle than those who let fear override their mind and mental faculties.** This is not to say that successful leaders don't have negative thoughts on the result of their plans; they do, but they take control of their fears and cater for any adverse eventuality which may arise. At the end of the day, *the degree to which you can control these two emotions is largely dependent on your training, emotional quotient, the extent to which you have generated confidence in your command, the camaraderie and morale of your organisation and the deliberation with which you have planned the operation.*

Lieutenant General **Mohinder Puri**, PVSM, UYSM (Retd), was commissioned into the Third Gorkha Rifles in June 1966. An alumni of the National Defence Academy and Indian Military Academy, he had held various command and staff appointments in the field and at the Army Headquarters. In the Kargil War 1999, he commanded 8 Mountain Division which spearheaded the Indian counter-offensive against Pakistan, capturing Tololing and Tiger Hill which became household names during the War. He superannuated in April 2006 as the Deputy Chief of the Army Staff. He has written a book, *Kargil: Turning the Tide* which is a first hand account of the War.

6

Mentorship and Grooming

A Solemn Responsibility

Syed Ata Hasnain

Mentoring is something that can be done successfully by anybody who has experience. However, perceptions about mentoring differ and hence the need to commence this with a definition. The internet definition appears quite comprehensive and appropriate. "Mentoring is to support and encourage people to manage their own learning in order that they may maximise their potential, develop their skills, improve their performance and become the person they want to be". Making the process of learning much smoother and faster on the basis of experience and value of lessons could be added here. This is all about getting people fired up and made capable of achieving the moon. It's a part of leadership. Not in a momentary situation but over a period of time.

All you need is a mentor and a mentee. However, it can be a little more nuanced, with multiple mentors and mentees, group mentoring or just simple role modelling. The role of the mentor in any of these is to nurture the mentees, encouraging them to learn, grow and upskill through their career, while aiming high. This can be formal and structured or on a personal note through emerging relationships. Leadership is one domain which can be learnt or simply refined through mentoring. It consists of principles and skills that are accessible to anyone and everyone. They aren't necessarily intuitive, but they aren't terribly difficult, either. So, one may study leadership as a subject, various theories and explanations about it and try to imbibe traits of past or present leaders. However, if you have someone available to you in flesh and spirit, whose traits you admire and whom you can communicate with, the beginnings of mentoring and mentorship already exist. It's then a question of establishing a relationship and then following it up through two-way communication, although mentorship can also be a one-way communication; less effective of course and more like role modelling. Perceptions on mentoring, its methodology and worth will always be based upon personal experiences. However, a mentee emerging as a mentor himself will probably lead to a win-win situation for all.

I have believed in the worth of mentoring through my career and beyond and continue to mentor and be mentored nine years after superannuation; it never comes to an end and never should because there is no end to learning either. In the Armed Forces it is the art of leadership which is most appropriate for learning through the mentoring process. In a forty-year-long career in the Indian Army I was constantly seeking and receiving mentoring or always mentoring someone, a collection of people or just individuals with whom I established a more intimate bond. While professional soldiering is highly complex from a learning and career point of view the principles of mentoring are ideally suited to it. One undergoes tenures of two to three years and attends courses of duration three months to a year. This is ideal for establishing mutually respectful relationships which support the mentoring process. Formal structures of mentorship and mentoring do exist in the Army so it's a question of interpreting the entire idea from your own point of view or with some guidance. The institution of the Colonel of the Regiment is actually a formal structure of mentoring. How it is exploited and interpreted is up to the Regiments, their officers and the prevailing environment. Let me analyse my own career experience to arrive at some conclusions.

At the beginning of my career, I was unaware that I was subconsciously being mentored all the time. Some of those mentor-mentee relationships lasted forever and continue till today. Talk at a personal level to any old-time soldier or even the current stock of senior serving or recently superannuated officers and you are bound to be informed about how they grew in service learning from weathered and experienced warriors. With the Army's concept of 'passing it on', I recall that at every stage of my service I had someone to look to for advice when I was stuck with life's options or simply situations I could not clearly comprehend. Elderly Junior Commissioned Officers (JCOs) of my unit and experienced Company Commanders were always available to advise on the ropes of better man-management, weapon handling and small-scale tactics.

Settling into the profession of soldiering is a great challenge. Everything seems important and everything seems your business, so time management itself is a challenge that one has to overcome. If you have no ego and no qualms about who you learn from, the cycle of learning and imbibing will become a part of your life. I remember watching detachments of specialist weapons working with one or two unit officers for their pre-course training. I was then reasonably far from being nominated for the Battalion Support Weapons (BSW) Course since there were seniors who had not yet attended. It was an NCO from our unit who gave me advice that I could join the pre-course training squads whenever I had the time. I followed that advice and under his guidance mastered the 81 mm Mortar, 106 mm Recoilless Gun (RCL) and the Medium Machine Gun (MMG) over almost three years. Subsequently I came and presented my Best Student trophy of the BSW course to that NCO and the set of soldiers who had seen me through that training. I maintained a mentor-mentee relationship with them forever. There were many things I taught them too, especially current affairs and J&K's history, while being deployed at the Line of Control. The relationship need not remain limited to one-way learning, it's competence based; you bring your competence and others bring theirs and the learning process gels.

The 1970s were the days when 21 officers were posted in an infantry unit; relationships were created on the basis of being understudy to someone senior, the senior subaltern system was in vogue and the JCOs commanded and received their own respect. Generations of officers who grew up being so mentored would recall the evenings in officers' messes and dinner nights; it is not for nothing that these practices were institutionalised; the mentoring and learning process was even greater at these occasions. These generations understood the value of mentoring and gave it back in equal measure to subsequent generations in their charge and then beyond. That is how Regimentation flourished and played such a great role in maintaining high standards; because senior regimental officers considered it their moral duty to pass on their experience. No political functionary and no civil servant can ever appreciate that and it will be a pity if the Indian Army ever does away with the Regimental system.

Unconsciously one develops a fascination for some personalities whom you wish to emulate. The relationship may never even be two-way. I recall that my first Brigade Commander was a fire eater, a stickler for high standards in everything. I admired his ability to be informal at one time and completely formal at another. Subconsciously over the years I seemed to be imagining him in many situations that I faced. How would he have responded? I wondered. That is subconscious mentoring which is unrealised at most times. An additional aspect of that subconscious mentoring is that you wish to maintain a certain standard in every domain; one which would find ready acceptance from a role model; the standard that he or she would have maintained. You do not want to let that person down because you imagine that he has a watchful eye and is constantly keeping a vigil over you.

The Army gives you the opportunity to serve with different personalities and then go separate ways but in the process certain relationships develop; sometimes due to affection and quirks of personality and many times due to a conscious effort. There is, for example, nothing stronger than a relationship between a military instructor and a student. That is because the Army picks the best to be instructors. In my case it started with the Junior Command course. I perceived each of my instructors as a role model and gave them all a kind of respect reserved only for those who are special; that relationship continued for many years. I did not seek anything tangible from it, a more subconscious type of relationship. At the Defence Services Staff College since the course was spread over a year one got to be seen better and had a greater experience of being under various instructors. There were relationships which lasted the career and continue today. I remember Lt Gen Shantanu Choudhry and Lt Gen Vinayak Patankar in their DSSC avatar. A degree of informality developed over the years and one could take the liberty to seek their advice at any time, as they too grew to be senior officers. It is this experience, as also with many others, which inspired the actions I executed while I commanded the Junior Command (JC) Wing in 2009-2010.

Commanding JC Wing was an experience which made me grow many years, although I was already a Maj Gen with 35 years of experience. I went to that appointment quite reluctantly, initially not very inspired by it. However, a certain introspection led to the conclusion that this was an opportunity of a lifetime. As Commander of the Junior Command Wing, I realised that I could make a transformational change in the ethos of the Indian Army through mentoring of junior officers, not just teaching. I took the responsibility beyond usual tactics and administration associated with the programme, allowing officers and their spouses to speak, write and discuss their ideas about life through an active blog on the internal information technology network. It was a learning experience for them and for me and my team of outstanding Directing Staff (DS). We realised what was going through the minds of the new generation and could tailor the education we were imparting through many discussions we had as a DS body. The mantra of 'relationships for life' was established here, delivering a message that relationships need not be transactional, for the moment or for the tenure. They must be transformational in outlook and forever. In the opening address and the closing ceremony of each course the message was delivered that JC learning was like a foundation course since all Arms/Services came together the first time after commissioning. Friendships would get reinforced but most importantly professional relationships would get established, both with the instructors who one took a fancy to and also with the peer group of colleagues. Many would pick study partners for the DSSC entrance exam based upon their experience of JC Course and even professional mentors to whom they could refer back. We introduced a brief symbolic gesture at the closing ceremony of every JC Course. It involved getting all instructors (45 of them) on the stage of the auditorium as the course stood to applaud them. It was explained that the *Guru-Shikshak* (teacher-student) relationship was one of the most sacred in Indian culture and needed to be nurtured as a relationship for life. I kept getting feedback on this through the DS body (instructors) and was encouraged by the positivity that this advice generated.

It is not enough to only motivate the potential mentee; the potential mentor must perceive that he too has the worth of being a mentor. It takes time before the motivation builds within both segments who are likely to have such a relationship. Towards this end a bit of tweaking of the JC Course syllabus gave us the leeway to find a few periods we could devote to a series called 'command experience'. Initially it commenced with the existing instructors and their wealth of experience and knowledge. Instructors from different Arms and command experience of different terrain or operational conditions, put together that experience into a 45-minute presentation with time for 45 minutes of interaction. Complete liberty was given to the instructors to remain as critical or appreciative of the system in vogue. This package was subsequently expected from every new instructor posted to JC Wing as he would normally be fresh from a command tenure. The feedback from the student body was that the learning value of one such event equalled almost a week's worth of theoretical learning and discussions. Since mentoring is all about passing on knowledge and values gained over time, this event managed to capture the right ethos. It helped the students identify those core competencies of their instructors that they wished to imbibe and learn. I am told many relationships flowered as a result of this initiative.

Guest lecturers in an institution many times lead to many ingredients of the mentoring system coming alive. That is why it is so important to select the guest lecturers with great forethought and application of mind. The JC Wing had no system of guest lecturers, so busy were the students in learning and relearning what they had done at the academy that there was no time for this. We experimented with Colonel (later Maj Gen) Yash Mor of the Brigade of the Guards, an officer who served in 36 Rashtriya Rifles (RR) in South Kashmir and took to CI/CT operations as a second nature. He had an easy style of communication and had done many small-scale operations. His lecture, repeated ad nauseum over many courses led to many officers taking to him in an off-the-course relationship, querying on practical aspects and role modelling on him. Today Maj Gen Yash Mor is a mentor to many in civvy street, helping bring the right human resources to the Services. The lesson: get iconic people, great communicators and ones with indisputable character as guest lecturers, to speak at all institutions and they need not be just senior officers. Many times, they strike mentor-mentee relationships.

As a student my finest experience was the Pre-Staff College Course at Mhow, then run by HQ Central Command. It's there that I came across some of the finest instructors with whom I struck up a lasting relationship well beyond just the initial success of passing the DSSC Entrance Exam. These relationships lasted many years and were most productive from a learning point of view.

In a slightly different context, I wish to highlight a form of mentoring which came very handy for my command while I served as a Corps Commander in the operationally highly active environment of XV Corps in J&K. I am describing this primarily because I perceive that the worth of mentoring does not apply only to structured and formal ways. Over passage of time and with experience I realised that situations in Kashmir hardly ever change.

They mostly return in cycles of a few years; the past methods being often repeated. Units, however, serve three years at the Line of Control or on the CI/CT grid. Officers command units for a year to three years and command of brigades and divisions is for a much lesser tenure. There is a lot of institutional learning among formations that is passed on to units, but what is available in the form of personal experience, distilled through years of maturity is something special. Yet, very few commanders or COs ever pass on the nuggets of their experience. What is hurriedly put down on handing and taking over notes is about all; the real experience is taken away in the mind. That is what we wished to exploit through a simple structured system. We directed that all COs and brigade commanders would be in touch with three to four of their predecessors. In the case of COs, it meant identifying COs of units which had served at their location, ascertaining what rank they were at and where they were serving. For RR COs it was easier as the predecessors were from the same unit and brigade commanders too found it easy to pinpoint their predecessors. We requested that an informal relationship be established and a regular interaction be followed to ascertain the activities and lessons of a particular time in the past. It helped establish positive relationships, forced the past officers, many of them at more senior ranks, to introspect and feel the worth of their own tenures, and pass on that experience. For those then serving in the operational environment of Kashmir it was a boon, some great advice on offer and also the ability to establish a 'one on one' with personalities who they may never have come across or had opportunity to serve with. It was mentoring of its own kind.

It would be sacrilege to attach motive to mentoring, although for some it is definitely a means of social climbing. It has a great role in the promotion of ethics, values and morals. Role modelling is important in this domain, the silent way of communication but it can also be a very conscious effort at nurturing within corporate organisations, through the setting up of formal hierarchies for mentoring.

When it comes to formal hierarchies the Army is one organisation where structures for mentoring can be set up in a practical and doable way outside the formal command channels. This can especially be applicable in Infantry regiments where the Colonel of the Regiment may wish to decentralise and set up informal hierarchies under some senior officers of the Regiment who then act as mentors to a set of units. Although viable, this does not guarantee the level of success which voluntary link-ups offer.

The coming of social media and easier forms of communication through the information revolution has facilitated mentoring in no small way. Mentors and mentees can be in more frequent touch, be more cryptic or detailed in communication (generally acceptable on social media) and also involve in mental communication through public jottings, messages on personal pages and broadcasts. I do this with a host of officers who share their ups and downs with me on a regular basis. It's an important part of my post superannuation activities; the proverbial 'giving it back' responsibility which drives many of us. It gives me the greatest profit that life can offer, the profit of satisfaction that one has friends everywhere.

Cut to the situation today. There have been incidents galore involving officer-man relationships leading to unsavoury situations and a blot on the Army's otherwise flawless record. Much of it comes from the immaturity of officers who are expected to realise the limits they can go to. No doubt, we have educated and aware soldiers who do not fully understand the value system of the Army but equally you have officers who have been unfortunate never to have been mentored in the art of man-management, regimentation and officer-man relationship. While this is a generalisation it is equally important to mention that there are regiments and units who do it extremely well even today. Strong regimentation and involvement of even the veteran community, irrespective of rank, marks the informal system and continues to spread the culture of correctness.

Do veterans have a role in mentoring? I would say most certainly. Shorn of responsibility of appointment, veterans have the time to reflect on their experience and cull out the necessary parts which can be put to great use. They may have to reorient themselves a little and remain current in the world of professional developments which rapidly move forward, needing flexibility and much focus. To some veterans this comes naturally especially if you have tenanted instructional appointments through service. A veteran's ability to mentor also depends on the spoken reputation he acquired while in service. A negative reputation will not be helpful even if you try to change from your earlier avatar.

Principles of Mentoring

This essay would be incomplete if one just ended with the experience of mentoring as explained above. It's important to arrive at certain principles outside textbooks. These will be useful in adopting mentoring, as a mentor or a mentee, at any stage in life. Here are some principles as identified on the basis of my experience. Readers can add much more to this based upon their own experience.

No Restrictions. It starts with the very important principle that there is no age or gender bar. There isn't a restriction on mentoring remaining limited to commonality of profession between mentor and mentee. It's all a question of intellectual attraction and ability to gel between them.

Goal Identification. Informal mentoring, which is the usual method we follow in the Armed Forces, must also have some goal identification. The mentee and the mentor may establish their own individual goals. However, if a formal mentoring process is established the goal identification must be done in consultation, for best results.

Trust, Familiarity and Awe. To maximise learning and imbibing what's up for takeaway, trust is an important factor. When one trusts implicitly one is involved with the heart and in a transformational way. Familiarity is great; it breaks barriers of communication but redlines must be known to all. The aspect of 'awe' is important, yet also debatable. If it inspires fear then awe is not a suitable inspiration; high respect is a more appropriate sentiment which will inspire mentoring far more effectively.

Knowledge, Experience and Maturity. The quest for knowledge is one of the aspirations of mentoring. In fact, mentees seek out mentors on the basis of General Knowledge, Domain Knowledge and the nature of experience. A hands-on experience coupled with effective communication is something that mentees revel in. At the same time, to make these abiding relationships, the base level of knowledge of a mentee needs to be at an acceptable level. If I am a mentor, I can't be expected to be interacting with kindergarten knowledge in my domain. The mentee must display the right maturity to make a success of the relationship. Many a time a mentee progresses in rank and acquires status equivalent to the past status of the mentor. The furtherance of such a mentor-mentee relationship would depend on the maturity of the mentee and how he handles his own success. Ideally nothing should change.

Transparency and Feedback. Trust automatically leads to more transparency. Yet transparency also contributes to enhancing trust. Interaction in writing, verbal communication or face-to-face dialogue is helpful in providing free and frank feedback while remaining in deference to rank asymmetry. The mentor must act as a sounding board and not always seek congruence of thoughts with a mentee. Disagreement and its acceptance is also a part of such relationships. Managing differences of opinion is a special responsibility of the mentor.

Focus on Specialisation. Both generic and specific domains remain important in mentoring. Lasting mentorships usually depend on diversity of domains and levels of interest of both mentor and mentee.

Networked Mentoring. In the world of modern social media being part of multiple networks is common. There could be group, or one on one mentoring. Either way mentoring through social media must proceed as per some norms as most exchanges tend to be in the public domain. Mentoring in the military profession is preferable in a private one on one mode or through a social media medium, or through emails. It is possible to mentor and align the thinking of many young mentees (outside the military fold) in a geographical area where there is a need to play out our narratives; I am referring to the many young people in J&K with whom our officers establish relationships. This is a subject by itself and this kind of mentoring has a slightly different set of norms.

Self-Learning/Development. The military profession attracts a lot of focus and attention due to a certain degree of romanticism attached to it. Many young people come on board to get inspired and also learn. All of them do not necessarily join the military profession. Even if there are many young people just attempting to be mentored for their self-development it's a phenomenon which should be welcomed and veterans in particular can be involved after ascertaining some basic security norms of social media. It helps to temper the existing social environment where the spread of the values of the Armed Forces only helps to positively inspire more people.

Expectations from Mentoring. These must remain within the realm of reason and never be unfettered lest it leads to huge disappointment, low morale and a psychological setback. A mentor must also make it clear as to the space up to which a mentee can enter. Hand holding is always possible in deserving cases but till a point.

In the Armed Forces the disciplined upbringing, hierarchical respect and distance, and norms of behaviour actually make the entire exercise of mentoring more effective without any overstepping. However, the one thing I always attempt to adopt is a restraint from 'sermonising' and an attitude of 'I am OK, you are not OK'. I often recall that most of the initiatives which I undertook in my service at various stages of decision-making, were actually never my own ideas. They mostly belonged to some subordinate commander or staff which got associated with my name. That actually gave me the perception that there are out there, among our subordinates, hundreds of very capable men and women who only need encouragement, a slight hand holding and a pat on the back; with just this they can achieve the moon. It's our task as mentors to ensure that they achieve the moon because that is what mentoring is all about.

Lieutenant General **Syed Ata Hasnain**, PVSM, UYSM, AVSM, SM, VSM & BAR (Retd), is a former General Officer Commanding of the Kashmir based XV Corps. He inspired learning in the Indian Army through the adoption of the US initiated Scholar Warrior system. A prolific writer he continues to be a public speaker and strategic analyst making many complex issues easier for the understanding of the public.

7

Civil-Military Interface to Optimise Leadership

AK Singh and SM Kumar

Introduction

Leadership is present in all walks of life, be it the political, bureaucratic, corporate, or military field. Whilst for all others it is equally important, for the military, leadership is it's "core business", which will often make the difference between victory and defeat, between life and death. Although this book is largely devoted to leadership in the profession of arms, yet military leadership at the senior levels cannot be looked at in isolation, ignoring the other instruments of state and the corporate world which have much to offer.

The prime focus of this chapter is to analyse the differing perspectives and imperatives of leadership between the corporate and the military, to identify the threads and concepts which can be harmonised. This will enable the optimisation of best leadership practices, for the benefit of both—the civil and the military.

The armed forces the world over, including in India produce some outstanding leaders, who lead men in some of the most challenging and risky situations. The leadership attributes they possess, and practise are of course critical to the armed forces; these are also much cherished and sought by our civil counterparts, particularly those in the corporate world. Qualities like integrity, courage, selfless devotion, and decisiveness, with a high quotient to function in an ambiguous and disruptive environment, would be equally valuable on the civil side.

Teamwork, trust, and ownership are the bedrock of military leadership, to build an environment where the individual merges his/her aspirations within the organisational goals. These are the same qualities sought by the corporate world. It's unfortunate that in India, this missing interface deprives some outstanding military talent from enriching the corporate world, especially at the middle and senior levels. A few who make this transition have made a name for themselves, but a vast majority of military leaders who retire are wasted out.

Similarly, the armed forces can pick up some of the best management practices from the civil side, especially in the field of resource optimisation and exploitation of disruptive technologies. Even human resources (HR) practices followed by mature business organisations are imaginative and agile, and in tune with the changing times; the armed forces can certainly benefit from their examination and adoption.

The corporate world has borrowed many leadership concepts, strategies, organisational structures, decision-making processes, contingency planning, and crisis management models from the military. The corporate world has refined many of these concepts, married them seamlessly with emerging technologies to improve efficiency and result-orientation. They have reached a level of maturity and agility in many fields, where military leaders, as also bureaucrats, can learn a lot from the corporate world.

In fact this cross pollination of ideas and practices is already happening in the advanced nations and it is high time we empower our leaders in India to benefit from the same. This chapter is an attempt to do just that.

Part I. What is so Special about Military Leadership?

The Indian Armed Forces are the ultimate guarantors of the Nation's security and well-being. How this instrument of last resort performs will be determined by the leadership that steers the organisation in peace and leads it in war. While leadership is present in all walks of life, what makes it so unique and special in the context of armed forces is due to the undermentioned aspects:[1]

- **Unlimited liability covenant** (unwritten) between the organisation and individual, where you give yourself up to the armed forces and carry out the assigned duties without any ifs and buts! In return, the organisation and the Nation commit to looking after you and your family in life, injury, or death. This is a unique and treasured two-way bond that only exists in the armed forces.

- Leadership in the armed forces is not about profit/loss but involves life and death issues. Therefore, the motivation must be on a higher plain and leaders must lead through personal example/influence, both direct and indirect, to make their command achieve the seemingly impossible.
- Being the last resort of the nation, must win every time, time and again—there being no prize for runners-up in war.

The armed forces function in an environment that is apolitical, secular, and diverse without any distinction based on caste, creed, region, or religion. Professional merit is the major criteria for advancement, without being subject to various pulls and pressures, as is prevalent in the civil side. Having control of their promotions and postings, the armed forces are relatively immune to the political pulls and the pressures that the bureaucracy and other services are routinely subjected to.

Serving in the armed forces is a "**calling**" whereas in the corporate world it is business. Notwithstanding the differences, much good is possible in understanding and imbibing the best practices of both.[2] Discipline, loyalty, trust, ownership, and ethics (to name a few) followed in the military, can be complemented by creativity, innovation, and optimisation of resources and disruptive technologies in the corporate world.

The concepts of military leadership are so universal and powerful, that most civil organisations in the developed world, have not only adopted these, but gone a few steps further, in refining and harmonising them with emerging technologies to optimise the end effect. However, in India we are more focused on adopting leadership and management models churned out abroad, without benefiting from what is available within. Cynicism about the other side has become a roadblock that is yet to be overcome.

In the 21st century, threats and security concerns are no longer confined to silos and are not just the concern of the armed forces alone. Non-traditional threats like water and food security, health issues including pandemics, mass migration, livelihood and skilling, environmental degradation and many other contemporary challenges require a wholesome approach involving multiple stakeholders including the government, the industry, the academia and the military. The requirement therefore is to harmonise and synergise our concepts and capabilities for optimum effectiveness. There is no other way.

It is also necessary to disabuse a widely prevalent notion that all defence expenditure is non-productive. The defence forces are intimately linked to the national economy, not only for ensuring a secure environment, where business enterprise and individual genius can flourish, but also for driving the vast military-industrial complex, where dual-use technologies are widely used. Every year approximately 75,000 military personnel, including many in varied leadership positions, retire and join society; unfortunately, we in India are unable to tap into this disciplined and multi-talented HR pool, which is tantamount to a gross waste of precious national resource. Both the government and the corporate world can benefit from utilising them.

The military's main charter is to prepare for war and conflict in all dimensions. The leadership principles and concepts they follow have a universal application across governments and civil organisations including the corporate world. It's time we capitalised on what the military has to offer, by enhancing mutual interactions to create a win-win situation.

Harmonising and Optimising Best Leadership Practices

There is much to learn from each other as far as best and relevant leadership practices are concerned. Some of the key issues are analysed below:

Vision and Core Values. What does the organisation stand for; what values do its employees embody; how does its output/products contribute to the nation and society at large? Whilst the armed forces have a clear set of core values, the corporate sector has often shown expediency in defining and pursuing their core values, for short-term gains. No wonder that today in terms of credibility, the citizens trust their military the most. Even in the armed forces, the core values are sometimes under stretch, as has been argued elsewhere in this book, though the institution has by and large stood firm. The corporate sector must realise sound ethics makes great business sense, and that a dishonest and hollow set of values will not get you far. There are many examples from Satyam Computers to Kingfisher Airlines and Harshad Mehta to Nirav Modi. The stakeholders in the corporate world are narrowly defined, but the bottom line is to ensure competitiveness and to create value for the shareholders. To this should be added "brand reputation" and "core values" which will better define the organisation, rather than the balance sheet, profit & loss and cash flow statement alone. In our view a set of the following attributes should always be part of the core, apart from some others:

- Integrity and transparency
- Responsibility-Authority-Accountability
- Diligence and perseverance
- Gravitas not expediency
- Loyalty to various stakeholders including the customers.

Building Trust and Ownership. There is an official hierarchy in the military, but you also work with your team members in an informal way to understand each other and develop trust. When you take charge as a leader, there is a reputation that precedes you. However, it's your day-to-day actions, especially when the chips are down, that have a major impact. Your teammates are quick to notice:

- Are you self-oriented, or do you give priority to the organisational objectives and the team?
- Do you stand up and be counted in crisis situations and for your decisions?
- Do you apply the same standards to yourself that you expect your organisation/teams to follow?

In the military, trust and ownership are key components towards mission accomplishment. Ownership and trust also go hand in hand; ownership not only for the direct responsibility, but even for those indirect things that may impact the mission and the end result. There is much that the corporate world can imbibe from the military.

Decision-Making. In the military, 'decision-making' is both a science and an art. For every situation a military leader is confronted with, a decision becomes imperative within his arc of responsibility and even in the area of influence. Whilst directives and orders would be passed at appropriate levels of command, these do not and cannot cover every contingency. The military leader is therefore trained in the art of decision-making through an operational appreciation, which is quite scientific in its approach, covering all factors that may have a bearing to arrive at possible courses of action and finally the course adopted, which leads to a plan of action. However, time and inputs being always at a premium, military leaders also learn the art of taking decisions in an uncertain environment, without waiting for all inputs (The 70-30 Principle). Here, the military leader is greatly assisted by his **intuition** which he develops through his professional military knowledge and experience gained through imaginative training. In fact, many organisations are already benefiting from the training methodologies and the professional education followed in the armed forces, both for the individuals and team building. Such training also enables a common ethos and doctrine, where an organisation can function through 'Directive Style of Command', with minimum instructions. Some developed countries take their military officers to stock exchanges to learn how traders make decisions in split seconds under time pressure. With advancements in open-source intelligence (OSINT) and artificial intelligence (AI), machine learning (ML) and deep learning tools and technologies, smart decision-making in a human-machine environment has become imperative for both military as well as business leaders.

Risk Taking. Play safe and a *status quo* culture is out of sync with the dynamics of the 21st century. Leaders, therefore, must lead the change and accept the risks that this may involve. This is inherent in most tasks undertaken by the military in an operationally challenging environment, where decisions taken may mean the difference between victory and defeat, life and death. But in the armed forces, even risk-taking is a well-thought-out action, where the leader has measured the pros and cons and, more importantly, has also worked out contingency alternatives, should that risk-taking falter. It's not a toss of a coin, as some may believe! Therefore, recognising and seizing the moment is the art of superior Generalship, developed through intuition for risk-taking. Military history is replete with numerous examples of success achieved through calculated risk-taking. Business leaders can learn much from military leaders of today as well as yesterday. Similarly, in the business world, leaders like Steve Jobs, Jeff Bezos, Elon Musk, Bill Gates, Jack Ma, Dhirubhai Ambani and Gautam Adani have been known to take risks; when these pay off the dividends are out of proportion for the stakeholders.

Part II. Leadership in the Corporate and Entrepreneurial World

The previous section focused more on military leadership and how the corporate world could benefit by drawing upon leadership lessons from the military.

This section talks about leadership in the corporate and entrepreneurial context.

The element of "fog of war" and glorious uncertainties of the battlefield have always impacted military thinking and leadership principles. The volatile, uncertain, complex and ambiguous (VUCA) world in which business leaders of today operate and the pace at which disruption is occurring, makes their operating context analogous to the battlefield. Then there are issues that impact nearly everyone on the planet—like the pandemic and climate change.

The technological and budgetary edge that the military once so clearly enjoyed is also dwindling. Big technology (big tech) is investing heavily in R&D. Areas like space exploration which used to be the domain of the state are now being encroached upon by large global corporations and ambitious entrepreneurs too. Areas of friction between the governments and big tech are emerging, with US regulators focusing on anti-trust, EU on data privacy and security, and China reining in big tech with a massive crackdown.

The Pandemic Reinforced the Importance of Leadership

This decade seemed to be beginning on a note of promise—the global economy was recovering, and stock market indices were at an all-time high. However, things turned southwards rapidly. The twin shock of the global pandemic and economic dislocation nearly turned the world upside down. The lockdowns, travel bans, resulting uncertainty and crisis put extraordinary demands on leadership. The once-in-a-lifetime crisis exposed inadequacies in organisational leadership and business continuity plans. The crisis threw up new opportunities, leaders, champions, and innovators. Several innovative digital, born-in-the-cloud start-ups emerged during the pandemic; yet others scaled rapidly to become unicorns (start-ups with valuation of over one billion dollars).

There are many parallels between military and entrepreneurial leadership; albeit there are subtle (and some not so subtle) differences as well. Sub-section 1 will bring out the subtle differences, as well as highlight similarities.

Sub-section 2 would enlarge upon the qualities required of corporate leaders (beyond what has been talked in Part 1 of this chapter about military leadership). These include agility, authentic leadership, empathy and humility, ability to cut through clutter, innovation, resilience, storytelling, etc.

Crisis separates good leaders from the average. When times are good, even donkeys look like horses. Sub-section 3 talks about crisis leadership.

Pursuing entrepreneurship in a developing country like India is akin to fighting a war in non-linear battlespace, with battles of varying intensity on several fronts. Section 4 talks about 'Entrepreneurial Leaders', and why we believe, veterans can make excellent entrepreneurs.

Corporate Leadership in Times of Uncertainty

The World We Live In

We live in times of huge geopolitical uncertainty, socio-economic difficulties, an environment at a tipping point, a pandemic ravaging the world, great market volatility, rapidly shifting consumer preferences, blurring boundaries between work and life, network effect and 24×7 social media. Disruption and competition come from very unexpected quarters; garage-based start-ups are usurping long-standing sectoral and vertical leaders.

The VUCA world that we currently live in is explained by the following:

- The world is changing rapidly. It took Telephone 75 years to reach 50 million users, Radio took 38 years, Internet 4 years, WhatsApp, Instagram, Facebook, and Twitter took less than 2 years, Pokemon Go took only 19 days.
- The pace of technology-enabled disruption is accelerating—the implication is that either you embrace technology, transform digitally, or be prepared to become irrelevant.
- Business models are evolving—from pipes to platforms; new opportunities are emerging at the intersection of industries. Consumer preferences are rapidly shifting; digital transformation is all-pervasive.
- COVID-19 caused a double-whammy, an unprecedented health-care crisis and a massive economic dislocation. It also accelerated trends and put to severe test the leadership and crisis handling skills of business leaders and entrepreneurs.

Leadership and Management

In military, the term leadership is popular; in the corporate world, the term management is widely used. Much has been written about leadership and management, and we do not intend to reproduce them here, except a simple quote from the legendary management guru, Peter Drucker:

> "Management is doing things right; leadership is doing the right things."

Leadership is about getting things done. It is about sharing a vision, empowering, and motivating teams, creating a collaborative culture, and achieving the desired results. Anand Mahindra, Chairman of a leading Indian Conglomerate, believes that leaders must "envision, empower and energise."

Corporate vs Military Leadership: Many Similarities, Yet Subtle Differences

Corporate leadership is similar in many ways to military leadership. Business strategy and leadership seem to have drawn heavily from military best practices distilled over centuries and contextualised them to their unique operating circumstances.

Corporate strategy is concerned with long-term survivability and growth. Profit and loss (P&L) are important and last man, last round is not always the preferred option. Here, pragmatism trumps idealism. While duty, honour, country are the guiding principles for military leaders, corporates must balance these with the interests of their stakeholders. However, despite focus on wealth creation and profits, corporate organisations are beginning to attach great importance to purpose, values, culture, code of business ethics, policies, and processes. There is also an emphasis on assimilation of technology, data-based insights, and decision-making.

Historically, the most revolutionary technologies usually had military origins, and they were stripped down for civilian applications. However, over the last few decades, more technology-enabled innovations are coming from the civilian world, and some cutting-edge civilian technologies are being adopted by militaries the world over.

The corporate world has now become adept at the use of technology for innovation, management, and oversight. The Democratisation of technology has led to garage-headquartered, born-in-the-cloud start-ups daring to challenge and usurp global corporations.

Hierarchies to Networks

In the industrial era of mass production, centralised authority and hierarchy were important. On the production line, everyone had a well-defined role. Only a few managers needed to be aware of the big picture. Where you stood depended on where you sat.

As the world become more interconnected due to boom in civil aviation, mobility, telecom and internet, things began to get more complex. Relentless quest for higher efficiency and productivity led to globalisation of value chains—ecosystems, cross-cultural and cross-geography collaboration. Diversity, networking, outsourcing, and partnership became important. Sometimes, overemphasis on efficiency came at the cost of resiliency.

Armed forces have evolved and fine-tuned leadership and managerial principles over centuries—much of it has also been absorbed and contextualised by the corporate world.

As organisations became global and innovation and disruption cycles became shorter, the success depended more on creating a pool of leaders, diverse, empowered teams, cutting down hierarchies, building a collaborative culture, etc. The term servant leadership entered the lexicon—humility, empathy and communication became desirable qualities for corporate leaders.

Leadership Traits in the Corporate World

Principles of war and military leadership have applicability beyond the forces. Qualities that lead to success in military life are also useful in the context of business. Leadership, management, mission-orientation, innovation, resilience, collaboration, trust, teamwork, tolerance for ambiguity, contingency planning, and crisis management, which are germane to the military, are all valued in the corporate and entrepreneurial world as well.

Much of what has been written in Part 1 about military leadership is applicable in large measure to corporate and entrepreneurial leaders as well. In the paragraphs below, we shall cover a few important attributes which assume significance in the corporate world.

Agility

Agility provides the winning edge in a turbulent world. Agile leaders excel at absorbing information from their own experiences and then extrapolating from those to navigate unfamiliar circumstances. Such leaders are open-minded and inquisitive, have a propensity to seek improvements, are more willing to consider information that is at odds with their preconceived notions. In short, they are more willing to be different, and take risks.

Agility is built into the military organisation and doctrine. Agility and mission-orientation of a combat group or a battle group gives it the war winning edge.

As companies grow, they can become victims of their own bureaucracies, inertia, and risk-aversion. Maintaining strategic agility in the face of a successful maturity is a major challenge facing the CEO of today. Remaining agile would require robustness, resilience, responsiveness, flexibility, innovation, and adaptation.

Leaders like Steve Jobs (stay hungry; stay foolish) firmly discouraged mediocrity and rejected unquestioned acceptance of conventions. He exhorted young people to do new things, to go where others had not dared, try new ways of doing familiar things, experiment, learn, discover, invent, innovate, and achieve.

Agility also involves cost (a major consideration in corporate context). Requisite agility is a level that balances the costs of attaining it with the consequences of not having it. Learning agility or the ability to learn, adapt and apply ourselves in a constantly morphing world is equally important.

Authenticity and Conviction

Authentic leaders are comfortable being who they are. They let their actions speak for themselves, they lead the teams on the most difficult tasks.

Good leaders follow their convictions and passion, even when things are tough and not going as per script. They back themselves and do not give up.

Good Leaders Cut through the Clutter

Noise becomes data when it has a cognitive pattern.

Data becomes information when it is assembled into a coherent whole, which can be related to another information.

Information becomes knowledge when it is integrated with other information in a form that is useful for making decisions and determining actions.

Knowledge becomes understanding when related to other knowledge in a manner used in anticipating, judging, and acting.

> Understanding becomes wisdom when it is informed by purpose, ethics, principles, memory and projections.
>
> —Dee Ward Hock, Founder, Visa Corporation

In the era of endless connectivity, 24×7 news channels, hyperactive social media, Twitter, WhatsApp, WeChat and Instagram, fake news almost always outpaces the real. For every narrative, there is a counter-narrative. Information overload and excessive noise are a reality of the times we live in. This further amplifies during crises situations. Good leaders have the skill and intuition to find patterns in the noise and put together bits of seemingly unrelated information to build a picture.

Good military and corporate leaders read developing situations very well. They read fragmentary information and weak signals accurately and determine patterns. They define the problem statement well and focus energies on clearly identified priorities and core issues to achieve desired outcomes.

Culture and Empowerment

Culture is the way things are done in an organisation. "Culture eats strategy for breakfast," said the management guru, Peter Drucker. Culture is important in both the military as well as business context. Leaders in large corporate organisations create leadership teams, empower them, and set them up for success. They create a collaborative, high performance, values and rules-based, data and metrics-driven culture.

Mission Command

Military principle of "mission command", where you give broad objectives to the subordinate commanders, allocate resources, empower them, and leave the interpretation of ground realities and execution to the field commanders, is equally relevant and practised in spirit in large global organisations, though terminologies may vary.

Execution

Ideas are a dime a dozen, execution is everything. Great leaders, whether civil or military, excel at execution.

Empathy and Compassion

Good leaders demonstrate empathy and compassion, particularly to colleagues impacted by adversity. Good leaders lead with a combination of heart and mind.

Humility, Self-Awareness, and Diversity

Humility is about knowing who you truly are. Good leaders know their strengths. More importantly, they know their weaknesses.

In the corporate world, good leaders know what they know, what they don't and what else they must try to know. They monitor the evolving situation closely and accordingly revisit strategies and decisions.

In progressive organisations, leaders often select their team members with complementary skills. Diversity is considered a strength and an organisational and societal obligation. Good founders carefully select co-founders and core team members with diverse skills and competencies.

Health and Fitness

As per World Health Organisation (WHO), health is a state of complete physical, mental and social well-being, and not merely the absence of disease or infirmity. This is something which is taken for granted in the military. But, outside as well, great leaders work hard on their health and fitness, despite travel across time zones and busy routines.

Focus

Do less to do more. Success in the business world requires laser-sharp focus on your core competencies and sharpening your competitive edge. Great leaders are good listeners and ask the right questions. It is akin to the principle of war called "Concentration."

Growth Mindset and Innovation

Gemma Leigh Roberts in an article titled, "Why all great leaders need to be lifelong learners" explains:

> "... in a working world, where the pace of change is faster than ever and the half-life of any skill is about 5 years, one of the most important things a leader

can do is to be a constant learner... The best leaders learn from experiences—including failures—apply those lessons to unfamiliar situations in the future. They see challenges as opportunities as opposed to threats, proactively seek knowledge to stay up to date in a rapidly shifting professional environment and are curious to identify areas for development and try new ways of doing things.

"They have ... a 'growth mindset', which is the attitude and belief that we can all improve our skills, abilities and emotional intelligence with time, effort and energy. Leaders who are constant learners are open to change based on fresh opportunities, as well as needs of employees and customers.... People with growth mindsets are better at dealing with change, solving problems, successfully implementing and giving feedback, and accomplishing goals."

Innovation

Jack Zenger and Joseph Folkman in an article in *Harvard Business Review* on December 15, 2014 titled "Research: 10 Traits of Innovative Leaders" highlight that such leaders display *excellent strategic vision, have a strong customer focus, create a climate of reciprocal trust, display fearless loyalty to doing what is right for the organisation and customer, put their faith in a culture that magnifies upward communication, are persuasive, excel at setting stretch goals, emphasise speed, are candid in their communication and inspire and motivate through action.*

Resilience

Business continuity and resiliency have been much-talked about concepts in the business world, particularly during COVID-19 times. Business continuity planning (BCP) is akin to contingency planning in the military.

Resilience is not only the ability to survive but thrive through challenging times and bounce back strongly; having redundancies, robust, tested contingency or business continuity, incident and crisis management, and IT-disaster recovery plans. Modular operations, multiple revenue streams, scenario-based planning (including preparing for worst-case scenarios), succession planning, and agile ecosystems strengthen organisational resilience. Responsible organisations and good leaders step up to help government and communities in times of need.

But do remember, building resilience takes time, effort, investment, and leadership commitment.

Storytelling

Great leaders communicate their vision through compelling stories. Religious scriptures have great stories. Political, military and business leaders are usually great communicators and storytellers. Entrepreneurs who are seeking to raise funds should be great at sharing and getting across their stories to investors.

Timing

Good leaders and successful entrepreneurs have an amazing sense of timing. They do not let adversity or distractions cloud their judgment. Timing may be the difference between success and failure. Bad times are not necessarily bad for innovation and enterprise.

Corporate Leadership during Crisis: Much to Learn from Military

A crisis puts additional demand on leaders where military leadership lessons have great applicability in crisis situations.

Timely and accurate intelligence is vital in evolving situations. In crises times, when there is little or too much information (as is often the case in the social media age), acting on vetted, reliable information in a time-sensitive manner is critical. Progressive organisations have evolved intelligence gathering and analyses mechanisms; they also share a summary of facts and implications with their employees.

Each crisis is unique and requires different kinds of resources and expertise—in a pandemic, you need doctors, in a hurricane you need generators and communication, in a flood you need boats, sandbags and food. Yet crisis leadership requirements, managerial skills and supply chain principles remain abiding.

Denis Waitley said, "Expect the best, plan for the worst, and prepare to be surprised."

Leaders must stay strong and calm, keep their heads clear, make decisions based on available facts, organise, improvise, plan, communicate and oversee implementation under chaotic conditions.

Good leaders, in both civil and military, put up a core team to deal with emergencies, and facilitate quick decision-making and rapid responses.

Crisis communication is extremely important. More than 50 per cent of crisis handling is communications. During COVID-19, employees in organisations got a lot of conflicting news and had many anxieties. Some suffered personal losses. Corporate leaders in good organisations remained in touch with their people explaining the situation to them, giving them clear directions to enable them to overcome anxiety and to perform to potential. Communications included those regarding business continuity and continued delivery of services to customers, keeping supply chains functional, travel (restrictions), remote working and work from home policies, certainty regarding jobs, pay and allowances, health needs of families and social responsibilities.

Never Waste a Crisis

A crisis is also a good time to introspect and effect long overdue changes. COVID-19 helped focus government attention on fixing the broken health-care system. The pandemic also threw up lessons for organisations—big and small. Lessons from each crisis must be identified and institutionalised by the leaders to be able to handle the next one better.

Crisis throws up leaders without titles, stars, stripes or designations, who rise to the occasion, refuse to give up and inspire those around them to accomplish seemingly impossible missions. Such performers must be recognised.

After the Crisis

Every crisis has a beginning, a peak and an end. Some like earthquakes or tsunamis strike with little warning, others with some warning (floods and hurricanes), and those like pandemics come with some warning, but can have long-term and devastating health and socio-economic consequences.

After the crisis, it is important that leaders:

- celebrate the work done well, giving credit to the team
- accept responsibility for the shortcomings
- Learn from mistakes
- Bring them to formal closure.

Entrepreneurial Leader

Leadership in a start-up or entrepreneurial environment is even tougher. You must stay long enough in the game to be lucky.

Entrepreneurship, in many ways, is like a war in a non-linear battle-space, with many near simultaneous mini battles of varying intensity and complexity. An entrepreneurial leader requires many of the military traits to succeed—belief in the cause, mission orientation, concentration (focus), agility, flexibility, reserves and a multitasking aptitude.

Many people want to become entrepreneurs to make money, to get rich and famous. When people are in a corporate job or working in a government organisation, we (in our own heads) do tend to overestimate our individual contributions and underestimate the value that the organisation or brand brings. The truth gets exposed only when you start up on your own.

Samuel Pierpont Langley was an American astronomer; a pioneer of aviation; he wanted to be the first to fly. He was a graduate of a top college, had impressive work experience, was funded handsomely by the US government, hired the best team money could buy and was followed by the leading American newspapers. The market conditions were just right—the aviation boom those days was like the dot-com boom. Langley had the recipes for success—great idea, brand, buoyant market, capital, and team. Sadly, he quit attempts to fly when someone else succeeded.[3]

Then, there were the Wright brothers who made the maiden flight and created history on December 17, 1903. Their team had little formal education or degrees, the mission was funded largely by proceeds from a bicycle shop.

Why did Langley fail? He was perhaps driven by the wrong causes—be rich and famous; he hired guys who wanted secure jobs and fat pay cheques.

The *mantra* for success is not money, market conditions or team alone; the "WHY" is important. It must be pursuing a cause that attracts other talented, capable professionals. That is why the Wright brothers succeeded in flying with literally no funding, supported by a team with no formal degrees, but with a missionary zeal that they were working to change the course of human history.

Entrepreneurship involves a fundamental mismatch between resources and ambition. Entrepreneurs, like skilled military leaders, set their ambitions and sights high, use their scarce resources well and achieve more with less.

Entrepreneurs must have a powerful idea. They must use technology, teams, capital, and resources optimally and efficiently to find solutions to big problems. Be distinct or extinct; differentiate or die.

Entrepreneurship involves risks, much like military missions. Entrepreneurs must take calculated risks and not be afraid to fail. However, remember to FAIL FAST so that learning costs are minimal, and you stay alive to fight another day.

Focus. Much like the military principle of concentration of force at the point of decision. Entrepreneurs must concentrate their energies and resources on the most critical tasks. **Do less to do more.**

Team. Entrepreneurial success is almost always a result of teams and individuals with complementary skills working together in mission-mode to achieve the near impossible. Bad hiring is among the worst mistakes corporate leaders and entrepreneurs can make. The Military has a wonderful time-tested and rigorous selection process all along the hierarchical ladder.

Entrepreneurs must remember that **Cash is King**. Sound advice in entrepreneurial life—"**top line (revenue) is vanity, bottom line (profit) is sanity; cash is reality**." Businesses die mostly because of cash flow issues.

Let Go. As in military, delegation and empowerment is critical. Someone has rightly remarked, "graveyards of the world are full of people, who thought they were indispensable."

Ethics and Values. Much like military organisations, great entrepreneurial organisations can only be built on sound ethics, values and well-defined and implemented code of business practices. Even though being **GOOD** may be challenging and difficult, it's the best way.

Conclusion

For the military, leadership is its "core business", which will often make the difference between victory and defeat, between life and death. The corporate world has borrowed heavily from the military in aspects of leadership, strategy, organisational structures and processes; they refined these, married them seamlessly with emerging technologies to improve efficiency and result-orientation. Cutting-edge technological innovations, once the preserve of the military, are coming increasingly from the business world.

In conclusion, it would be fair to say that military leaders, bureaucrats, corporate leaders and entrepreneurs can learn much from each other.

Veterans can make excellent corporate leaders and entrepreneurs as they possess in abundance the star qualities required for success therein.

Some takeaways for the 21st century leader:

- Leader-Manager rather than manager-leader.
- Visionary, decentralised, intent-based, empowering leadership with an ethical focus.
- Possessing high tolerance for ambiguity.
- Disciplined, loyal, cost-conscious, selfless, and courageous (qualities associated with military commanders) should be complemented by the corporate leader's relentless result-orientation, quest for value creation, creativity, innovation, use of disruptive technologies and risk-friendliness.
- Above all, the 21st century model is about influencing, empowering, building relationships and unleashing creative energies. It is also about synergising individual aspirations with the organisational goals through compassion and a combination of the heart and mind.

Notes

1. Essence of the armed forces; Ch 1 of the book, Lt Gen AK Singh and Brig Narender Kumar, *Battle Ready for the 21st century* (Delhi: Pentagon Press, 2021).
2. Panel discussion on "Transformational Leadership in Changing Times", CDM, Secunderabad, July 23, 2010.
3. Excerpted from a famous TED talk about Samuel Pierpont Langley and the Wright brothers.

Colonel **SM Kumar** (Retd), is an alumnus of IIM Calcutta, King's College, London and Joint Services Command & Staff College, UK. Col SM Kumar (Sam) is an experienced Security and Risk professional, with a demonstrated history of building and driving business to profitability & sustained growth. Founder CEO of MitKat Advisory, a leading Asian risk consultancy, and currently its Managing Director, Sam leads the development of products to achieve its mission—*"de-risk client business and protect vital assets"*. Sam is an acknowledged thought leader, speaker and author. He appears on prime time TV, Radio, security and leadership conclaves, and supports veterans and entrepreneurs.

8

Leadership Challenges in Uncertain Operational Environment

VK Ahluwalia

"In an uncertain world, senior officers must be the leaders of change in the profession of arms …"

—Marin Corps General Joe Dunford, 2019[1]

One Who Dared Ambiguity

Soon after the Partition of India in August 1947, the situation in the Kashmir Valley presented a highly uncertain, complex, and ambiguous situation between October 24 and 27, 1947. On his return from Kashmir on October 26, when Lord Mountbatten, the last Viceroy of India, asked Colonel Sam Manekshaw (later Field Marshal) about the military situation in Kashmir, Manekshaw pointedly responded saying, "Very bad, Sir." He further stated that once the tribesmen get into Srinagar and the airfield, we (India) would lose Kashmir. This thinking of Manekshaw led to the nomination of 1 SIKH to move into the Kashmir Valley, and induction of additional troops to follow. "Uncertain environment" was all too evident by the sketchy intelligence and ambiguous tasking of 1 SIKH, that was personally drafted by Lieutenant General Sir Dudley Russel, the newly appointed Western Army Commander. Excerpts of his operational Instructions notes:

> […] Tribesmen, numbers and arms unknown but reliably reported to be in large numbers, are reported moving to Srinagar … You will:—(a) Secure Srinagar airport and civil aviation wireless station; (b) Take such actions, as

> your first task and available troops allow to:—(i) Drive tribesmen away from Srinagar;...

Lieutenant Colonel Ranjeet Rai, CO 1 SIKH, was handed over these operational instructions with two sets of maps at 0300 hours on October 27, at the airfield in Delhi. There was extraordinarily little that the CO and his Paltan (Battalion) could do to plan and prepare—even the information was too ambiguous to plan anything.

On reaching Srinagar in the early hours, the CO deployed his defence platoon to secure the airfield. Thereafter, given the prevailing grim situation, he was faced with the dilemma of his next course of action, especially when the communications with Delhi were difficult, and the information of the tribesmen and the raiders was all too vague. Given the gravity of the situation and many options that came to his mind, he finally homed onto two possible options: First, to occupy defences close to Srinagar; and give a good fight, with additional reinforcements and artillery that would fetch up the next day or so. Second, to meet the raiders as forward as possible and to blunt their advance to Srinagar. Possibly, the CO realised that an uncertain environment is a double-edged weapon—that can either destroy or provide a battle winning opportunity. In an extremely uncertain and unpredictable situation, with scant information available about the raiders, Lt Col Ranjit Rai took the most bold, proactive, and offensive decision to challenge the raiders, even with a relatively small force. He went as forward as Baramulla, where the raiders had paused to loot, plunder, and rape. Losing no time, he moved his battalion to the outskirts of Baramulla to prevent any further advance and thus, saved the Valley from falling into the hands of the raiders, and in turn to Pakistan. It was a classic case of excellent leadership which exhibited tolerance for ambiguity, proactivism, and seizing the opportunity offered by the uncertain situation. He interpreted the operational instructions and the intention of the Army Commander in the best interest of the country.

Therefore, uncertainty is directly linked with risk and an opportunity to take action. It allows the proactive force to get into the observe, orient, decide and act (OODA) loop of the adversary—thus making him react. John Boyd had designed this decision cycle to ensure effective decision-making in the midst of an uncertain environment or chaotic conditions.[2] Although Lt Col Rai had less than 12 years' service, he was faced with the most uncertain operational environment. His quality of leadership stands as a perfect example in terms of: comprehension of the situation, quick decision to move ahead, and gain a position of advantage by taking the enemy by surprise.

The paper aims to analyse the fundamental sources of uncertainty, illustrate with a few examples, and suggest actions to be taken to prepare the leaders and troops to operate in an uncertain environment.

Geopolitical-Economic-Strategic Interests

Two centuries ago, the Prussian General Carl von Clausewitz mentioned that, "War is an area of uncertainty.... The first thing (required) here is a fine, piercing mind, to feel out the truth with the measure of its judgement."[3] While answering a question about the evidence of Iraq government supplying weapons of mass destruction (WMD) to terrorist groups, Donald Rumsfeld, the then US Secretary of Defence, explained the term "Unknown unknowns".[4] In the modern days, "unknown unknowns" is a common term in strategic planning and project management. *Business Dictionary* defines it as: "Future circumstances, events, or outcomes that are impossible to predict, plan for, or even know where or when to look for them." Uncertainty in an "unknown unknowns" situation is perhaps the worst form, as it is neither possible to plan nor is the probability of outcome foreseen. Under such circumstances, one is not sure what would actually happen. Therefore, the aim should be to get requisite information to reach a stage of "unknown known", and finally "known known", if feasible.

One of the biggest recent examples of challenges to leadership in an uncertain environment was experienced in the Russia-Ukraine war that commenced in late February 2022. Despite the digital-cum-information age, most of the information available in the initial stages was highly unreliable. TV shows and social media had churned out endless narratives, and a plethora of articles were written based on one's perception or national interests or geopolitical alignments. Psychological warfare was at its best! The situation remained uncertain and ambiguous. Therefore, awareness of geopolitical-economic-strategic interests and their cross term impact needs to be clearly understood by the leaders at appropriate levels, to join the dots.

Operation Neptune Spear

Among several examples of leadership's role in an uncertain environment, and at the highest level, was "Operation Neptune Spear". Post 9/11, it took almost a decade for the US to get some authentic information about the whereabouts of Osama bin Laden. In August 2010, Leon Panetta, Director CIA, announced, "... *the intelligence is not going to get any better. ... We must act now*". Following the trail of Osama's courier Abu Ahmad el-Kuwaiti and inputs from other intelligence gathering means, the CIA located Osama and homed onto a compound in Abbottabad (Pakistan), close to the military station. Considering the probable impact of such an operation in Pakistan, the US President Barack Obama, while seeking more information about the al-Qaeda Chief, demanded that various options be examined. As a result of which, by January-March 2011, four options were generated and debated, that entailed: One, bomb the compound; two, a drone strike on the compound; three, a helicopter assault on the compound, employing the US Special Operations Forces (SOF); and four, a joint operation be carried out by the US and Pakistan. Of which, the last option was ruled out without much consideration given the secrecy would have been compromised at the earliest opportunity, among other reasons.

It was an operation to be conducted in an extremely uncertain environment, with a huge political fallout at home and abroad. In the final meeting, 48 hours before Operation Neptune Spear was to be launched to kill Osama bin Laden, President Obama posited: "... *In the end, it is fifty-fifty that he is there.*" Here, one can draw a link to that of Colin Powell's famous statement: "Leaders should take a decision when they have 40-70 per cent of the information required for taking that decision."[5] Thus, President Obama gave the "Go ahead" with limited information.

A night before the launch, the Commander of the Operation asked his SEAL Team what the worst case in the operation could be. To this query, the youngest SEAL is learnt to have said, "*The helicopter may crash in the courtyard itself.*" This contingency was also discussed briefly, and correctly managed when it actually happened on the ground the next day. Thus, the operation, fraught with inadequate intelligence and unknown reactions, was carried out successfully by the SEALs with Joint Special Operations Command (JSOC).

These two cases put forward three important messages: First, uncertainty prevails at all levels—strategic, operational, and tactical. Hence, decision-making is required at each level. Second, decisions by leaders in an uncertain environment are a function of professional competence and knowledge, experience, confidence in oneself and his command, and finally, the 'intuition'. Third, under uncertain conditions, soldiers look up to their leaders and not managers. These examples also amply reiterate the fact that more often military leaders will be faced with lack of adequate information/intelligence, disruptions, and an uncertain environment. Even at the national and global levels, rapid changes in the geopolitics, economics, technologies, strategic and security landscape, coupled with lack of communication/engagement have increased turbulence and uncertainty in relations. All professional soldiers must remember what Major General Kem reiterates, "... *environment often rewards clarity and punishes those who wait for certainty.*"[6]

VUCA: Uncertainty is the Mother of Them All

Of the term Volatility, Uncertainty, Complexity and Ambiguity (VUCA) that was coined in 1987, "Uncertainty" is the mother of them all. The pertinent queries that demand attention are: What are the fundamental sources of uncertainty? How should one prepare for an uncertain environment which gives surprises, unpredictable and unknown outcomes?

To answer these questions, the factors that call for setbacks in the approach are as follows:

- **Lack of Information.** One of the primary sources of an uncertain environment is lack of information or intelligence about the situation or of the adversary. It would depend upon the credibility of the sources of information and the ISR capabilities based on: primary or secondary sources, credibility of qualitative or quantitative inputs, and effectiveness of communication system to disseminate to the most appropriate recipients. There was a huge air of uncertainty in 1999 due to inadequate information about the Pakistani intruders on the Kargil Heights, and the ability to deal with them. Information void leads to incorrect assessment and appreciation, wide range speculation and whisper campaigns. If adequate inputs are not available, the decisions could be entirely wrong, and lack of timely action also leads to greater uncertainty.
- **Organisational Uncertainty.** Environmental or the organisational hierarchical structure is also fundamental to creating an uncertain and

unpredictable environment. It occurs due to lack of uniform policies in human resource management, lack of transparency, operational experience, and inconsistent commitment to organisational goals; and unpredictable social factors like complex interpersonal relations, incompatible behaviour styles, and inconsistent method of sharing information. If the lower formation and unit commanders in the hierarchy are neither trained nor empowered with latest information to analyse and take decisions, not only will the operational commanders miss the fleeting opportunities but will create fear and apprehensions in the rank and file.

- **Conventional Mindset.** Most of the commanders tend to maintain a conventional mindset in an environment of unrestricted warfare, which "manifests in different forms".[7] To support this argument, it would be pertinent to quote Sean McFate who posited, "*Despite the West and the US having the best troops, training, equipment and technology, they have not won a war since 1945. … It is because of the mindset of 1945.*"[8] Resistance to change is the biggest hurdle in human behaviour. If we do not change our mindset to the challenges of the future, we will certainly continue to face uncertain situations to our disadvantage. With hybrid threats and disruptive technologies being employed by state and non-state actors and the resultant uncertain conditions, the commanders would be required to analyse the operational environment against time. Resultantly, the doctrines, strategy, and training philosophies remain embedded to conventional concepts. Given the rapid changes in the geopolitical-economic-technology-strategic-operational domains, there is an urgent change to keep pace with the 'speed of change', to remain proactive and gain a position of advantage.
- **Leadership.** If the leaders are not professionally competent and confident, uncertainty takes the better of them. Depending upon the level—strategic, operational and tactical—the leaders should be fully aware of the geo-strategic realities, the envisaged threat profiles, 4th Industrial Revolution and its impact, cross domain operational effects and essential military attributes. These are covered in the later part.
- **Focus on SWOT.** Lack of focus to carry out an objective SWOT analysis of the enemy, especially underestimating the enemy, results in uncertain and unpredictable situations. The endeavour should be to identify the

gaps, seek information, and join the dots to carry out SWOT analysis at different stages of operations.

- **Mission.** The leaders do not set out clear-cut goals and objectives (mission) and/or disseminate to subordinate commanders. During the operation D-Day (Operation Overlord on June 6, 1944), there was tremendous uncertainty as the airdrops of men and material of the Allied Forces went to the wrong places. Despite the initial setback, it was the "commander's intention, focus, and flexibility" which enabled the forces to fight through the fog of uncertainty.
- **Tolerance for Ambiguity.** The other factors that hinge on the fear of failure and zero error syndromes are low tolerance for ambiguity, and the culture of not accepting a divergent or contrary view. While President Nixon, the US President, was threatening to intervene in the 1971 war in East Pakistan, Lt Gen Sagat Singh took a bold decision to cross the Meghna River, and organise airdrop of a parachute battalion at Tangail behind the enemy lines. This action was taken against an ambiguous-cum-uncertain situation. It caught the Pakistan Army by total surprise—the most critical factor—and thus, resulted in the capture of Dhaka in an early time frame.
- **Technology.** The unwillingness to keep abreast of advancements in technology, its application, as well as to learn lessons from the past after action reports. Revolution in technology has brought in devastating power in the weapon systems, whose effectiveness can cause huge confusion and uncertainty. Technology has also changed the manner in which decisions are taken. It would be prudent, especially for the senior leadership, to remain abreast with the technological advancements and their applications.

Corporate Governance: A Study on Strategic Leadership

A study by PwC on strategic leadership in a corporate system in 2015 suggested:

> They lack people in positions of power with the know-how, experience, and confidence required to tackle what management scientists call "wicked problems".[9] Or the will to challenge the status quo, or to fight uncertain situations.

With a sample size of 6,000 senior executives, the study revealed that only 8 per cent qualified to be strategic leaders. The study also suggested that strategic leaders are more likely to be women, and that the number of strategic leaders increases with age.[10] It noted that besides the abilities of the strategic leaders to lead transformations, they are also adept at managing uncertainties. Therefore, the strategic leaders must keep abreast with the changing geopolitical, economic, technological, and strategic landscape, as it helps to astutely analyse the emerging strategic environment. It also helps to analyse the strategic risks, their impact, and the strategic choices available to deal with under a given situation in a proactive manner. Therefore, it is important to task and seek information to fill the gaps in the intelligence picture, to convert "unknowns to known". Based on the envisaged strategic environment, which need not necessarily always unfold in the same manner, the commanders must set the clear-cut goals and objectives and disseminate to their commands. In fact, the considered operational plans must be challenged by another independent team. This very practice would arm the strategic-cum-operational commanders to manage uncertainties and unforeseen contingencies.

To note, General George S. Patton, the famous general of the US Army, once said: "*Never tell people how to do things. Tell them what to do and they will surprise you with their ingenuity.*" Cases in point are Lt Col Ranjit Rai, MVC, and Major (later Lt Gen) Ranjit Singh Dyal, MVC! However, in practice, the commanders seem to forget this very dictum when they are faced with operational situations.

One of the important fundamental assumptions for war planning as propagated by Admiral Joseph Wylie suggests: "We cannot predict with certainty the pattern of war for which we prepare ourselves."[11] More importantly, the place, time, force levels, objectives are difficult to predict. Here, a case in point is the Vietnam War. Wherein, despite its massive advantages in troop numbers, technology and financing, the US could not predict with any accuracy what could be the next move of the North Vietnamese. The US's lack of information created a feeling of doubt, uncertainty, and confusion both in the armed forces and general population, eventually forcing America to withdraw.[12] This leads to the lesson that commanders must act in time to dilute the impact of the prevailing uncertainty. One of the ways to fight the prevailing uncertainty is to keep commanders and troops informed of the situation, to the extent considered appropriate.

While in the Indian context, historically, Indian Armed forces have taken a few proactive actions, manoeuvred, and gained a position of advantage against the enemies. Some of the prominent examples include: in 1948 in Jammu and Kashmir, General Thimayya's orders to move Stuart light tanks (7 Cavalry Regiment) to the mountainous Zozila (11,600 feet) to fight the enemy; Major Ranjit Singh Dyal's relentless actions to capture Haji Pir Pass in August 1965; in 1971 War, 4/5 Gorkha Rifles battalion was audaciously heli-lifted across the Surma River, south of Sylhet to isolate it; a large force of 57 Mountain Division was heli-lifted across the raging Meghna River in 1971; and 2 PARA battalion of the Parachute Brigade was airdropped at Tangail, an important communication centre, to capture the Poongli Bridge on the Jamuna River (which expedited the fall of Dhaka). Notwithstanding these incidents, Indian Armed Forces have generally been reactive, cautious, risk averse, indecisive, and status-quoists in their actions, save the recent actions to occupy strategic heights in South of Pangong Tso in August 2020. In fact, given the conditions that prevailed after June 15 when 20 Indian Soldiers, including a Commanding Officer, were killed, our actions to occupy strategic heights in the Kailash Range, though highly successful, were rather delayed. In a reactive scenario, it is imperative to note that an operational situation results in lost opportunities, and subsequently, the same operation would require much greater resources, and above all, success may not be assured.

Boots on the Ground

In several cases, as one can argue, uncertain and ambiguous conditions are created by us. The facts being the leaders are not in sync with ground realities. To substantiate this point, it is proposed to illustrate an incident in the Kargil Sector. It is well known that Kargil, Tiger Hill and Tololing have been household names since 1999, in both India and Pakistan; though for different reasons. It is an extremely difficult super high-altitude terrain, with harsh climatic conditions. To prevent infiltration by terrorists into the Kashmir Valley, a few counter-infiltration posts were occupied by the forward battalions close to the LoC. In early November, it snowed heavily, blizzards followed, and created white-out conditions in the entire sector. Going by the previous incidents, the route of withdrawal (about 15 km long) of one of the counter-infiltration posts was known to be highly avalanche prone. As the local commander was away on leave, one of the posts was not withdrawn, and it was feared that it would remain isolated and cut off during the entire winter. During the winters, the post was not required from both operational or logistics point of view. It was an avoidable situation if decision was taken at the correct time to withdraw the personnel. Resultantly, it was then proposed that helicopters (MI-17) could be tasked to evacuate the personnel, weapons, and equipment from the said post. As the said Post was in close proximity of the LoC, it would have required contacting Pakistan's DGMO to facilitate evacuation by helicopters.

The Division was faced with an uncertain situation, having large ramifications. The commanders on the ground carried out aerial-cum-ground reconnaissance to analyse the snow levels and pattern in different valleys, avalanche prone areas, and the likely risk of avalanches. The snow levels were compared with the previous years, and the areas where avalanches actually occurred along with their frequency. Although white-out conditions prevailed due to poor weather conditions, it was soon realised that the snow level was in fact much lower than the preceding years. After seeing the conditions, based on the knowledge of the terrain, earlier experience, and intuition, the commanders decided that the post does not require any evacuation by helicopters. Therefore, the post personnel were directed to walk back along the known route. Having taken all precautions, the walk back was to commence after 2300 hours the same night. Additional radio stations were set up by the signal company's boys to always remain in continuous communication with the Party. Simultaneously, a rescue team with "avalanche rescue implements" was suitably positioned to act, if required. The movement of the Party was monitored continuously. Unexpectedly, the Party reached back at the base much earlier than the scheduled arrival, as the snow levels were much lower than reported.

This situation highlights two important lessons: First, lower formation commanders should be empowered to take decisions based on criticality of the ground situation. In the instant case, based on the prevailing weather conditions and that counter-infiltration posts are not required close to the

LoC during winters, the local commanders should have recommended withdrawal of the said Post in time. Second, commanders must move to forward locations to remain abreast with the ground conditions. Wherein, one of the best ways to diffuse the fears and apprehensions of an uncertain situation, the commanders must physically visit the affected areas and have their "boots on the ground" to recommend or to take decisions. As the truth is, by knowing the ground situation and the pulse of the men on the ground, half the battle would be won.

Measures to Fight Uncertainty

Planning for uncertainty is less dangerous than planning for certitude. To avert the uncertainty, the "to-do list" entails the following actions:

Convert Data into Knowledge. Lack of information or intelligence is central to creating an uncertain environment. As they say that "Knowledge is power", the commanders must aim to turn data into knowledge, and convert an uncertainty of unknowns into a known risk by plugging the gaps in information. This can be done by filling the gaps in the intelligence picture through a method of—collect, analyse, and disseminate. In addition, one should also rationalise the previous after-action reports based on their objectivity. In doing so, one must avoid biases based on the tendency to accept information with a preconceived understanding. To exemplify, by December 1967, the American leadership had received adequate information about the Tet offensive that the Viet Congs and the North Vietnamese forces were preparing for a major military campaign against major cities, including Saigon (now Ho Chi Minh City).[13] During the Buddhist holiday of Tet on January 31, 1968, over 85,000 Vietcong troops attacked nearly every major centre in South Vietnam. This information was rejected by the senior US commanders as it was not in consonance with their assumptions. Therefore, to address this folly in thinking and acting, the wisdom lies in challenging the received information and the likely plans by acting as devil's advocate. As rightly posited by General Patton, "*If everyone is thinking alike, then somebody isn't thinking.*"[14]

Plug Information Gap and Formulate Action Plan. In an uncertain environment, the most important thing is to plug the information gaps, as explained in Figure 8.1. In doing so, to anticipate the future, one needs to be innovative and creative in finding solutions, to seize fleeting opportunities.

Figure 8.1: Identification of Gaps to Formulation of Action Plan

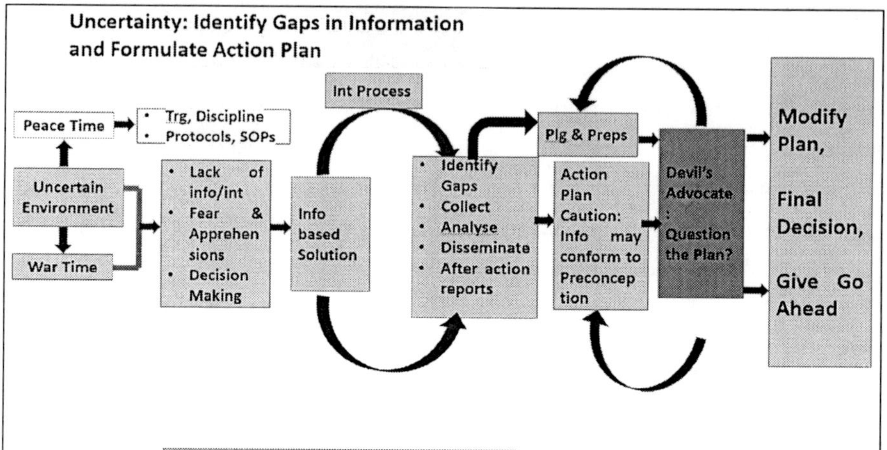

Source: Prepared by the author.

Communicate and Inform

In the midst of military operations, who is the most affected by an uncertain situation? While the answer may suggest many stakeholders, it is the commanders and soldiers in that order of priority, primarily due to anxiety, fear, and psychological stress of the unknown outcomes. Lack of communication results in anxiety, stress, and rumour mongering. Therefore, commanders must make a note of the findings of Stanford Research Institute, which suggests: "*Importance of understanding people and dealing with them comprises 88 per cent of leadership strategy.*" Therefore, keeping the men appropriately informed of the situation and the actions being taken reduces the impact of an uncertain environment.

When the chips are down, and uncertainty prevails, there is a tendency among a few leaders to isolate themselves. That is, rather than remaining open to people for information, suggestions, and diverse opinions, one seeks to adopt seclusion. But it is to be noted that good leaders engage purposefully with a large cross-section of people, and create a sense of togetherness by listening to a wide range of opinions. This helps better decision-making. *For, the cost of being slow in decision-making is often greater than the cost of being wrong.*

Leadership. With the threats having increased in scale, diversity and complexity, the leaders must be in grips with wide spectrum of threats: territorial-cum-boundary disputes, collusivity of threats by India's adversaries, militarisation of cyber and space, progressive increase in the roles of non-state actors, political objectives being achieved by non-military means or concealed use of military force, and role of information warfare to mould the perception of the population and armed force personnel to one's advantage. The leaders would do well to understand the impact of technology in achieving lethality, precision in engagements at long ranges, employment of swarm of drones in multiple roles, loiter munitions, and the role of disruptive-cum-innovative means of engagements. Professionally competent leaders are far more competent to handle uncertain and ambiguous environments; hence, they must be trained and put through varied contingencies.

Command and Control. One of the most important principles of war is to have an effective command and control system. However, it should not be interpreted as interference in the actions taken by the subordinate commanders. Simplistically put, the commanders would do well to simplify plans; spell out the intention clearly by way of a mission, train and rehearse the plan, and empower their subordinates to coordinate and take decisions, especially on situations arising in an operational environment. Here, 'resilience is the hallmark' of a good leader and the organisation—a few operational plans will always face unforeseen contingencies. Therefore, commanders must train themselves as well as their subordinates to aptly respond to the uncertainties.

Psychological Safety. Having coined the term "Psychological Safety", Prof. Amy Edmondson of Harvard Business School propagates that one will not be harmed or humiliated or punished for speaking with ideas, questions, concerns or mistakes. Only then can one expect continuous innovation for the betterment of the individual, the team, and the organisation. Besides conveying appreciation, the organisation and its leaders must provide multiple platforms for the individuals to express themselves, or to question the existing concepts and procedures.

Transparency and Critical Thinking. Depending upon the availability of time, the work ethos in an organisational structure should be based on transparency, participation, encouraging innovation, creativity, and critical thinking. This can be achieved by deliberate encouragement and push by the senior commanders. The commanders should give the broad direction to an operational problem, and allow the junior leaders to participate in analysing various options being discussed, wherever feasible.

Create Uncertainty for Adversary. When a commander deals with an uncertain situation, the orientation phase of the OODA loop is both the most important as well as the most neglected. Successful orientation requires a commander to destroy one's existing beliefs and create new ones based on the new inputs. Two quick examples of the corporate world that got inside their competitors' OODA loop, to make them react. First, the release of the iPhone in 2007 surprised everyone because it was unlike any previous smartphone: it combined an iPod with touch controls, a mobile phone, and an internet-enabled device. In 2014, Satya Nadella, the new CEO Microsoft, moved away from the traditional software products and created a dynamic cloud system solution for all end-users. Besides gaining huge competitive advantage, both these companies created a highly uncertain environment for their competitors. Similarly, military commanders must create a situation of uncertainty for the adversary, by being pre-emptive and proactive. As the GOC of the Division in Sikkim in 1967, Lt Gen Sagat Singh broke the myth of Chinese PLA's invincibility when he occupied the forward post on the watershed during the border at Nathu La.

War-game Contingencies. During the planning stage, various contingencies must be war-gamed, and the troops and commanders must also be trained to fight through the fog of war. That is to suggest, under uncertain conditions and lack of communications, standardised practices, procedures, training, and rehearsals come in handy, given the objective of the troops and commanders towards achieving a higher commander's mission. In addition, study of history, case studies, and after-action reports, with objective interpretations, also significantly facilitate decision-making by the commanders at different levels. Technology-based systems be also utilised to war-game different scenarios, and analyse own actions and their results.

Build Strategic Thinking

It is often said that the transition from tactical to operational levels of leadership is relatively easier than the transition to strategic leadership. What are the reasons? The tenures of officers at higher ranks in the Indian Army (Brigadier to General) are rather short, due to which they do not get adequate opportunities to think and plan at strategic levels. It is important that the officers must pay attention to professional military education (PME) as they grow in service, so that they understand the rapidly changing geopolitical-economic-strategic landscape, and its impact on national security. As the operational environments in the future would be uncertain, complex and ambiguous, the leaders would have to act in time to deal with challenges at different levels. While the leadership style of each military leader may be different, they must communicate effectively by reaching out to the appropriate level to bring clarity in the higher commander's intentions.

Given India's threats and challenges to its security, especially with over seven decades old boundary-cum-territorial disputes with two of its neighbours, and emerging threats from disruptive technologies, it should be prepared to act with speed. With an "all-weather friendship" between Pakistan and China, development of CPEC since 2015 through Gilgit-Baltistan region, and further strategic encirclement in place, India is faced with a new strategic environment—which is uncertain. Thereby, to avoid and quell the risks of uncertainty and get surprised by the adversary's acts, it is important to focus on a robust intelligence gathering system and build one's capabilities. While paying attention to inadequacies in institutional and organisational domains, it is important for the Armed Forces to adopt a dynamic approach to develop leaders at all levels, who are capable of operating in highly uncertain, ambiguous, and volatile environments. These actions would certainly facilitate faster decision-making and formulate an action plan to present an uncertain situation to the adversary.

> "*Victory smiles upon those who anticipate the changes in the character of war, not upon those who wait to adapt themselves after the changes occur.*"
>
> —Giulio Douhet

Notes

1. General Joe Dunford, Chairman of the Joint Chiefs of Staff; said during the graduation ceremony for the National Defense University Class of 2019.
2. John R. Boyd, "Destruction and Creation", 1976, at https://www.goalsys.com/books/documents/DESTRUCTION_AND_CREATION.pdf
3. Carl von Clausewitz, *On War*, 1835.
4. "What are unknown unknowns?", Definition and examples, at https://marketbusinessnews.com/financial-glossary/financial-glossary-u/unknown-unknowns/

5. Vidya Hattangadi, "The 40-70 rule of decision-making", April 27, 2020, at https://www.financialexpress.com/opinion/the-40-70-rule-of-decision-making/1940295/
6. *Strategic Leadership: Primer for Senior Leaders*, 4th edition (U.S. Army War College, Carlisle, PA: School of Strategic Land Power).
7. Qiao Liang and Wang Xiangsui,*Unrestricted Warfare, China's master plan to destroy America*. (Beijing: People's Liberation Army Literature and Arts Publishing House, February 1999).
8. Sean McFate, *The New Rules of War: Victory in the Age of Durable Disorder* (William Morrow, January 22, 2019).
9. PwC Study, "Ten principles of strategic leadership", 2015, at https://managersdo.com/en-10-principles-of-strategic-leadership-pwc-study/
10. Ibid.
11. Admiral Wylie, *Military Strategy: A General Theory of Power* (Rutgers University Press, 1967; Reprint, Naval Institute Press, 2014).
12. John Boyd, "The Ultimate Guide to the OODA Loop", at https://taylorpearson.me/ooda-loop/
13. "Tet Offensive Vietnam War", *Encyclopaedia Britannica*, 1968.
14. George S. Patton, at https://www.brainyquote.com/authors/george-s-patton-quotes

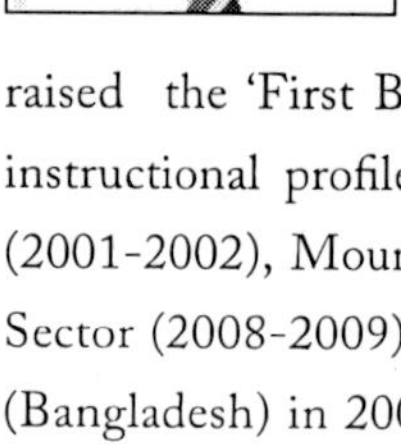

Lieutenant General (Dr.) **VK Ahluwalia**, PVSM, AVSM**, YSM, VSM (Retd), is Former Director, Centre for Land Warfare Studies (CLAWS). He retired as the Army Commander, Central Command in February 2012. Thereafter, he served as a Member, Armed Forces Tribunal (AFT), Jaipur. A keen Army aviator (helicopters), and a pioneer of the Bofors Gun system, he raised the 'First Battery' of Bofors in 1986. With a balanced command, staff and instructional profile, he commanded an Infantry Brigade in Uri-Baramulla Sector (2001-2002), Mountain Division in Kargil (2005-2006) and Corps in Leh-Ladakh Sector (2008-2009). He was the first Indian Brigadier to attend the NDC, at Dhaka (Bangladesh) in 2003. While commanding the formation in Kargil, his Division was awarded the BNHS National Green Governance Award 2005 by the Prime Minister of India on November 10, 2005, for conceiving and implementing the unique strategic concept, "**Operation Green Curtain**". He has also authored a book, *Red Revolution 2020 and Beyond* and edited three books on *Kargil, COVID-19* and *Bangladesh Liberation @50 Years*.

9

Junior Leadership and Role of Commanding Officer

The Key to Victory

Yash Mor

"It just takes one bad CO to destroy the hard work of three to five good COs in the life cycle of a unit."

—Gen George Patton, on command of a Battalion

The Indian Army takes tremendous pride in the fact that the junior leadership has always led from the front and has never been found wanting in any operational situation. The heroic deeds of young officers led by equally passionate Commanding Officers (CO) started well soon after independence. In the 1947-1948 warfighting, the first of the wars of Kashmir, the Indian Army equated it self very well due the courage of the junior leadership. The fact that Lt Col Dewan Ranjit Rai, was Killed in Action on October 28, 1947 while leading his unit 1 SIKH in the battle for securing the Kashmir Valley, is a testament to the commitment and zeal of the commanding officers of the Indian Army. In all operations post-independence, the steadfastness and the personality of the commanding officers have been reflected in the success achieved by the units. In the 1962 debacle too many units performed well where the CO stood tall, however many cases the units panicked when the CO was not up to the task.

The Army's leadership has been traditionally broken down into two broad categories, i.e., Senior and Junior Leadership. While senior leadership always denotes the flag officer levels, i.e., from Brigadier upwards, the term Junior level is used to loosely group everybody else from a Non-Commissioned Officer (NCO) upwards. And in this broad grouping, inevitably the focus is always on the NCO/JCO/Young Officer levels rather than the Commanders/ Commanding Officer's level. This level can be termed as the Middle Level and is the most crucial level of leadership, the grooming of which has always been neglected to a large extent.

It is at this level that the skill-sets of man-management and motivation come to the fore in addition to the earlier ingrained skill-sets of leadership and tactical acumen. As, with these ranks comes the command of a sizable body of troops (either a Company/Squadron or a Battalion). And each of these brings with itself its own unique set of challenges which are equal, if not more important than the challenges of leading a platoon or a troop in combat. More so, in an army of the nature of Indian Army, wherein the battalions/regiments are based on regional affiliations as well as to some extent caste lines, man-management takes precedence over everything.

Company/Squadron/Battery to Commanding Officer. The years spent in command of a sub-unit are crucial in shaping the promising and potential COs. This phase is very important as the connect with the men you command is perhaps closest in this part of an officer's life. All efforts must be made to "make this count". Too often this is either too short or spent in assisting staff in higher headquarters, specially if the Company Commander is already qualified on the Staff Course.

It's the duty of the CO as also the immediate formation commander to ensure that the command of a sub-unit is made meaningful and challenging. He must get full opportunity to be involved in all aspects of training starting from the Physical Training in the morning and always ending with a hard-fought games period in the evening. Outdoor training activities are great for bonding and an officer must take full charge of not only his men but also the equipment with which he is likely to take them to war. As far as possible there should be minimum disturbance and interference from the unit and higher formation.

The system and management of the career of the officer must ensure that a minimum of 4 to 5 years' time is given in this position. Too often we see the proverbial "Adequately Exercised" (AE) Major/Lt Col tag being used for upcoming officers to give them just bare minimum time before they are promoted and considered for the rank of CO. An officer who is not fully conversant with the challenges of command of a sub-unit often is found wanting in command of the unit. In order to sail ahead based on course profile, he is likely to avoid hard life in command of troops in difficult areas and seek better opportunities in peace or resort to firefighting to stay in the "good books" of senior hierarchy. The effort must be to ensure that even highly "qualified" officers must spend maximum time in the units in regimental duties.

Attributes of a Good Commanding Officer

It is not easy to define the correct attributes of a commanding officer. Most successful COs have had different ways and style of commanding. Many great commanding officers with huge success in military operations would have failed a typical peace tenure command! The same is also true of those who were bright during peace have had miserable failures in hard field or operational tasks. Notwithstanding this, let us try to see the basic attributes of a CO. Let us now try and define the attributes of a good middle-level officer, in command profile. These are must-have qualities for any CO, irrespective of the nature of the unit.

- **Physical Fitness.** Does not need any elaboration and is self-explanatory. He cannot be a burden for the unit to carry. The young COs of these times have no reason not to be seen along with men in PT and games. They must avoid the "old man" tradition gone with older generation.
- **Tactically Sound.** Warfighting is a serious business, where simple mistakes are paid for either in one's own blood or the lives of the men under command. It is not a matter wherein losses sustained in one quarter can be offset by the profits of another quarter, balancing the yearly P&L statements. Whatever be the nature or type of the unit, employment of his unit and its role in an all arms conflict must be clearly understood.
- **Morally Sound/Character.** A commanding officer has to be above everything. If the Subedar Major can be equated as the father figure of all the men under command, then the Commanding Officers' status is like a demigod. The men should worship him and be prepared to sacrifice everything on his command. Aspects of character include showing Army

values, empathy, warrior ethos/service ethos and discipline. The men may excuse any other weakness of a commanding officer but moral values and personal integrity don't go unnoticed.

- **Intellectually Sound.** A commanding officer should be well read, intellectually capable and be able to indulge in critical thinking. Innovation and problem-solving skills are of vital essence, especially in the Army's technical branches. With warfighting becoming more and more scientific in its outlook, knowledge of science, technology, engineering or math is becoming a norm even in Infantry units/battalions.
- **Leadership Skills.** The ability to lead under pressure is key for any officer. It is the most interpersonal skill—the ability to manage and lead other people, especially through tough situations. If he cannot relate with people and manage them when it's low stress, when it starts to get more difficult, it will be even harder for him. A large part of the leadership skill today is based on empathy, the troops need to see this side of even a hard taskmaster.
- **Personality.** Do not flap! Understand the effect your behaviour under pressure has on the sub-units and all ranks of the unit; this seems especially important to young COs of current times. You should be able to take a lot of load and instructions streaming in for the units almost on daily basis from higher formations. Having the courage and confidence to "ask the difficult questions", rather than ignoring difficult issues. At all times what counts is the moral courage by all officers, specially the CO. A personality who can make a fine balance between the demands of the organisation and his men, will be able to command without any rancour or prejudice.
- **Decision-Making.** One of the most important tasks for a CO is decision-making. If he makes quick and timely decisions, the subordinates have it easy. The CO must make decisions, be clear about what you want and communicate it effectively. Any sign of indecisiveness percolates to the rank and file, making them feel unsure of what is to be done. Listen to your subordinates and involve them in decision-making. This way the CO always inculcates a team spirit in the unit. This is also an important aspect of the Directive Style of Command (DSOC), which though encouraged on paper is seldom practised.

- **Developer.** It is important for a commanding officer to create a positive environment, develop others and steward the profession. He should be able to leverage, learn and develop individual skills and talents to get the job done using the right "mind-sets over skill-sets". He must make it a habit to give credit to his officers and JCOs for all achievements of the unit. He must personally take care to mentor his subordinates. He must leave a legacy of grooming a few more lines of succession not only for officers but also for JCOs.
- **Achiever.** All Army officers are expected to get results in their allotted roles. For commanding officers, it is not individual achievement which matters, but the achievement of his battalion/unit in all aspects. All COs need not be high achievers as we do need average regimental soldiers in command of fighting units, but on a personal level, the CO must be an achiever in any of his chosen fields of administration, sports, adventure training, etc.
- **Environment Management.** A good commanding officer should endeavour to create an environment conducive to the growth of the battalion. Without being overpowering in his influence, he must have the convincing power to ensure he is able to "shield" his command from the routine administrative tasks passed down from higher formations.
  - The career enhancement of all officers, JCOs and OR under his command.
  - Succession planning, look with a vision for at least one decade for the unit.
  - He must be able to balance between the requirements of non-core activities like the family welfare and ladies' meets. His better half too has a very important role to play, because, like it or not, she becomes the de facto head matron of the family. This is becoming a challenge today due to comparatively much younger age of the wives of the COs.
  - As much as environment management flows downwards, equal emphasis must be given to, not only up the chain, but also the lateral environment also.

In an army with rich traditions, a commanding officer also assumes the mantle of keeper of regimental traditions and its history. At the same time, he should be bold enough to change feudal traditions and customs continuing for perpetuity in the name of regimental tradition. In this he can be ably assisted and supported by the formation commander. The institution of Colonel of the Regiment can be a great help to the commanding officer in regimental matters.

In addition to the above, there are a few characteristic traits which become a must for any middle-level officer. These character traits will have a direct bearing, not only on the performance but also on the above elucidated attributes. These are:

- Confidence
- Directness, being frank and candid
- Discipline
- Team Player
- Courage, Loyalty and Integrity
- Respect
- Dedication
- Liveliness, the fun part in command.

Having laid out the traits and attributes of a Commanding Officer, let us have a look at the actions of some modern-day heroes, whose actions have immortalised them in the annals of Indian Military history. We shall study the actions of a few brave COs who laid down their lives in leading from the front, in the true traditions and ethos of the Indian Army.

Col Santosh Mahadik. A keen sportsman, he was a champion boxer, goalkeeper, and runner, he trained to be a paratrooper and a combat underwater diver. He was awarded a Sena Medal (G) for his daredevil ops in Kashmir Valley. Keeping his acumen in mind, he was nominated to command an RR battalion in *Kalaroos Jungles* of Kupwara District, probably the worst terrain for any kind of counterterrorist ops. Junior officers under him have described him as a leader par excellence, who always led from the front. He was martyred in a fierce gun battle with terrorists. Besides being a brave soldier, he was also an intellectual with a high degree of compassion towards the locals and their conditions. He was a keen environmentalist who wished more than anything to revive the natural beauty of Kupwara and revive tourism. A well-read officer, who took pains to reconstruct old monuments and build bridges with the local community. He felt revival of tourism was the way the youth could be given employment and diverted from radicalisation. He would personally counsel ex-militants and show them the path to a new life. In him, we see the characteristics of **physical fitness, bravery, empathy, compassion, education, etc.** His true character shone when in 2020, five years after his death, his classmates sent Deepawali sweets to his battalion. This act alone speaks volumes of his character.

Col Ashutosh Sharma. Yet another braveheart, who died leading from the front, Col Ashutosh Sharma was killed while leading a search party of 21 RR (GUARDS) to flush out terrorists hiding in Handwara, Kashmir. He was a **brave soldier** who has been awarded the Sena Medal (G) three times, a rare honour. Ashutosh Sharma wanted to join the Indian Army from a young age, and attempted to join for over six years. He was successful in his thirteenth attempt and joined the Officers Training Academy (OTA), Chennai **(Persistence to achieve goals).** A study of his profile will reveal **empathy as well as single-minded dedication,** amongst other qualities. He had been a company commander and unit second in command and had no reason to volunteer to command. But his heart was in soldiering and leading from the front. Incidentally this was the second incident in 21 RR, of a CO being "Killed in Action". This alone speaks volumes about the regimental ethos of the Brigade of the GUARDS.

Going back in time, we will now study the character traits of some of the famous middle-level commanding officers, who by their actions have left their mark on history.

Lt Col Dewan Ranjit Rai. Commanding officer of 1 Sikh, he was Independent India's first awardee of the Maha Vir Chakra. A bare study of his military profile will show the **intellect** behind the officer (he was the first Indian Officer to become an instructor at the Command and Staff College at Quetta). He was also selected for posting as military attaché to USA, when fighting broke out in 1947. **Leading his men from the front,** he was part of the first aircraft which landed in Srinagar. **In the absence of any command structure,** Lt Col Rai **seized the initiative** and successfully led his men on the Srinagar-Baramulla Road, deployed his men near Pattan and **successfully appreciated the situation** of providing depth defences to the airfield, paving the way for uninterrupted flow of troops and resources. In the little time at his disposal, he personally conducted reconnaissance and operations at such personal risk that he was eventually killed. By his **complete disregard of personal danger** and his **determined and inspired leadership,** he was able to save the airfield.

Lt Col AB Tarapore. As a young man, Tarapore was a keen sportsman, and was the school captain of a prestigious boarding school in Pune. Tarapore gained fame when he, by personal example, led his armoured regiment, the Poona Horse to victory in a series of skirmishes and tank battles in the Sialkot sector, always leading from the front, seizing initiative and exploiting opportunities. He launched an attack unconventionally, from the rear, surprising the Pakistani defences at Philoura. Inspired by his personal bravery, his regiment continued the attacks even after he was mortally wounded and created history. In him we see the characteristic traits of a good sportsman, leader who led by example, bravery and the ability to seize initiative and exploit a situation.

Military leadership, especially the middle-level leadership, is about doing the uncomfortable and being able to cope with it, overcoming powerlessness, and avoiding emotional breakdown. It demands a robustness in order to think clearly and effectively and to cope with one's feelings when facing complex and difficult situations.

Lt Col Desmond Hayde, MVC. Lieutenant Colonel Hayde was the Commanding Officer of the 3 JAT in the Western Sector, during 1965 Operations. On September 6, 1965, his Battalion captured the West bank of the Ichhogil Canal in Pakistan.

As part of Operation Riddle, 3 JAT was initially ordered to breach the Ichhogil Canal, which ran for 8 km inside Pakistan. The western side was lined with Pakistani concrete pillboxes that had overlapping arcs of fire. The Dograi township on the eastern bank of the Canal near the Grand Trunk Road was captured by the unit by 1100 hours on September 6, 1965. By 1200 hours on September 6, 1965, 3 JAT had captured Batapore on the west bank of the Canal despite stiff enemy opposition. It was for this action that Lt Col Hayde was awarded the Maha Vir Chakra. However, the battalion had to fall back as the other units detailed to support them in the offensive could not reach them in time due to a miscommunication. 3 JAT stood their ground alone until they were ordered to withdraw by brigade headquarters.

3 JAT then had to wait two weeks in defence at Santpura village in Pakistan before they were given orders to take Dograi, a town in the immediate vicinity of Lahore. By this time, the Pakistan Army had heavily fortified the town. On the night of September 21, 1965, during the impending attack on Dograi, Hayde made two demands of his men:

- *Ek bhi aadmi pichhe nahin hatega*! (Not a single man will turn back!)
- *Zinda ya murda, Dograi mein milna hai*! (Dead or alive, we have to meet in Dograi!)

3 JAT then marched 8 km from their trenches to Dograi, where the Pakistan Army had entrenched itself. The Pakistani force consisted of two infantry battalions supported by a tank squadron. Hayde warned his men against retreating by saying, "Even if all of you run away, I shall continue to stand on the battlefield alone."The battalion engaged in close-quarters combat, and eventually captured Dograi. However, 86 brave Jats were killed. The Pakistani casualties were close to 300.

Military history is filled with examples of how inspiring leadership at the command level has motivated the men under command to achieve superhuman feats of bravery in the face of overwhelming odds. As a contrast, history is also filled with examples of other self-centred, morally corrupt, time-passing, insipid and uninspiring leaders who have reduced great and reputed battalions to nothingness, forcing, in many cases the battalions/regiments to revolt and even to the extreme step of disbandment. In the post-independence Indian Army, we are lucky that we had a high quality of junior leadership and commanding officers. In all the wars since the first war over Kashmir in 1947-1948 till the latest stand-off against the PLA in Eastern Ladakh, this level of leadership has never failed.

In military history much has been said about how leadership of Generals turned the tide many a time. It's no one's case to dispute or deny this well-deserved accolade but there's very little which is spoken about leadership shown by CO and Junior leadership, including JCO/NCO sub-unit commanders in battle. National will is nothing but hollow words till the time it's enforced on the ground, and this, most of the times, is done by that YO/JCO-led Platoon or NCO-led Section, many a time without the supervision of a senior officer.

Remember, the Siachen Glacier was occupied by a daring team of Capt Sanjay Kulkarni (later retired as Lt Gen) and 29 men of 4 KUMAON between April 13 and 17, 1984. This team alone pre-empted the Pakistan Army from occupying the strategically important glacier. Also, it was the planning and initiative of Col Narender "Bull" Kumar since 1978 that we finally did what we did in capture of the Siachen glacier.

A wise general once defined the basic principle of a good Unit as "An organisation in which I knit, You Knit, We Knit. We all Knit together. Only then it becomes a Unit."

10

Trust and Ownership

The Essential Building Blocks

Anil Sengar

During the Arab Israeli War of 1967, there was an intense armour battle between the Syrian and the Israeli armoured brigades on the Golan Heights. The Israeli brigade commander gave a simple order to the Israeli armoured regimental commander, it said, "Stop that Syrian armoured brigade." Less than forty-eight hours later, the Syrian armoured units were in retreat.

In the military parlance, this is the finest example of what in the army is called the Directive Style of Command, which would broadly symbolise 'Trust and Ownership' as understood in corporate leadership. Here the superior commander lays down his intentions and broad parameters and leaves the methodology to the subordinate commander to accomplish the mission.

This brings us to the two aspects of leadership—Trust and Ownership.

Trust. Trust is a positive expectation that the other will not take advantage of you for personal gains. In an organisation, it is an expectation that you can be relied upon to deliver. It is a function of character, ability and demonstrated performance. From the subordinates' perspective, trust in the leader is non-negotiable for him to put in his heart. It is a two-way traffic.

Trust is a result of integrity, competence, consistency in behaviour, loyalty, and transparency.

Ownership. Relates to assuming responsibility and accountability for the accomplishment of the mission. It includes being positively proactive in attitude, decisive, solving problems, delegating, abstaining from blame, taking responsibility and regular objective reflection on events and their own actions.

Trust—Ownership Equation. With reference to the sketch below, the following equations emerge.

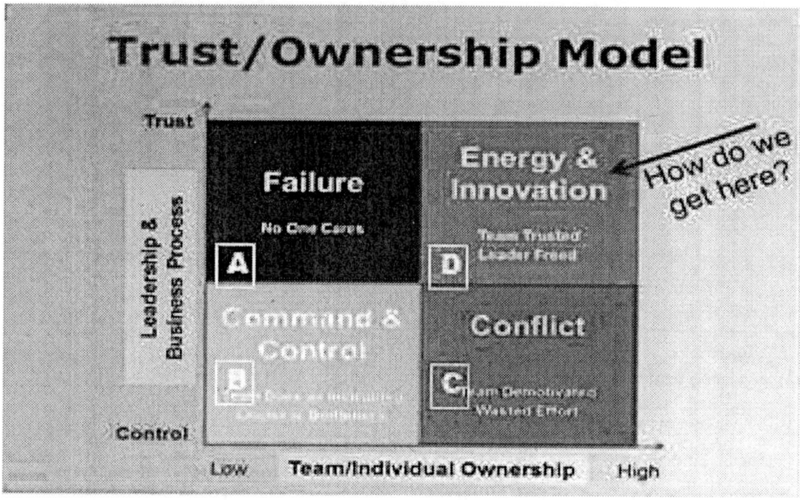

Source: Pollyanna Pixton, Paul Gibson, and Niel Nickolaisen, *The Agile Culture, Leading Through Trust and Ownership*.

Quadrant A. The leader trusts the team but does not delegate ownership.

- Leader trusts the team, but does not delegate ownership. The team will wait for decisions from the leader.
- It spawns lack of initiative and therefore slows down decision-making and progress. Results in further lowering of trust and slide into quadrant B.
- It is a centralised way of functioning that will create an inefficient organisation.

Quadrant B. The leader does not trust the team and does not delegate ownership. The characteristics of this quadrant are.

- Centralisation in functioning.
- Centralised decision-making and micro-management . Functioning based on detailed instructions on how and what to do.
- Managerial approach. Frequent status reporting.
- Transactional approach—reward and punishment.
- Passivity in approach. People do what they are told.

Quadrant C. There is a lack of trust for some reasons but ownership is higher. This is not a natural state and cannot sustain for long. It has to either upgrade to Quadrant D or slip to Quadrant B. The characteristics of this quadrant are.

- Frequent reporting and monitoring.
- Team will be asked to justify their decisions and actions.
- Lack of freedom of action and they would be falling back on the leader for approving their actions.
- Not sustainable, as accountability without trust will fracture the organisation.

Quadrant D. Leader trusts the team and its sense of ownership in functioning. Its characteristics are:

- The team enjoys the sense of responsibility and accountability because they have the freedom to choose how and why they function the way they do.
- The model generates momentum as the decision is pushed at the lowest level.
- Leaders do not get involved in what the subordinates are mandated to do.
- Delegation helps leaders to stay above the clutter to focus on the strategic issues that deal with the transformation and future readiness rather than on processes and procedures.

In any organisation, it is the human spirit which is at the centre of success. Human spirit cannot be exploited without trust and ownership. We have seen from the chart above that trust and ownership go together. One without the other is a recipe for failure and cannot sustain success over time. It leads to stagnation and failure to exploit the potential of the team. Thus the challenge for any organisation is to move from other quadrants to Quadrant D, which is the recipe for a progressive organisation. How does one do it?

Building Trust and Ownership

To arrive at how to build trust and ownership, it will be useful to examine the character of successful organisations. These are:

- Based on lasting values, where the stated values and the practised values are in congruence. Values define how its members are expected to conduct themselves from day to day. The values become the basis for taking decisions.

- The leaders, starting from the top, demonstrate adherence to the organisational values.
- Have a culture of free exchange of ideas and intellectual brainstorming where the hierarchy and positions do not come in the way of free exchange.
- Have an institutionalised practice of nurturing leadership at all levels and push the decision-making to the lowest level.
- Create an environment where its members have a sense of belonging, personal and professional fulfilment and enjoy each other's success.
- An environment that allows them to fail without becoming failures—accept mistakes committed in trying new ideas.

A leader is responsible to accomplish the organisational goals. These fall in two domains. First is to maintain the organisation's current viability and second is to prepare the organisation for the future.

A leader lays down the vision but it is the team that translates his vision into reality. It cannot happen unless the team sees it as its own vision and is fully engaged and committed. Getting them engaged is a function of the leadership. The basis for this is trust and willing acceptance of ownership.

A man's head is where his heart is and his heart is where his trust is. And trust is a two-way traffic between the leader and the led.

An organisation works at a number of lateral and vertical levels. A centralised structure kills initiative and delays decision-making. It sacrifices the benefit of multiple perspectives. Subordinates would have a tendency to kick the problems upwards for solutions. If the superior gives them solutions without getting them to exert themselves, he is not developing the ownership amongst the subordinates. This works against the culture of nurturing leadership. If a child falls and cries and you pick him up, the next time he will keep lying till you pick him up. Do not pick him up the first time, he will get up himself the next time.

Trust cannot be ordered or forced upon someone. Trust is a feeling as a consequence of what people see others do over a period of time, more when there is a price to be paid. Ownership cannot be forced beyond a point. Leaders cannot create trust and ownership by memos, rewards or punishments. It is a function of an enduring culture based on an enabling environment and a supportive leadership. The leaders can do so by creating that environment. The following guidelines will help.

- **Share Your Vision.** Help employees feel part of something bigger than themselves by involving them in formulating your vision.
- **Involve Employees in Goal Setting and Planning Activities.** Seek out their ideas, knowledge, and insights, and invite them to help make important decisions. Expose them to your process of making difficult decisions.
- **Explain the Why.** Making certain they understand *why* that task needs to be completed and *why* a particular individual has been selected for the job. Give the job a context in the bigger picture of your operation.
- **Let Them Choose the How.** Be certain that the desired outcome is understood and whenever possible, let your junior leaders decide *how* to achieve the task. This builds ownership in the process and stretches them to figure out a method for getting the job done. Give them credit and when they go wrong, ask questions that enable them to see better options rather than doing fault finding.
- **Delegate Authority, Not Just Work.** Give employees a leadership role. Leadership skills develop over time, and they require practice.
- **Trust Them Before You Have To.** Trust begets trust, ownership and accountability. Your trust in them will give them confidence, and that confidence is crucial to their personal development.
- **Encourage Them to Solve Their Own Problems.** Listen to their problems but don't jump in with solutions. Guide them through probing questions that will lead them to determine the right answer. When they get it, compliment them and make them believe in their ability and that you have faith in them to figure it out. Make them believe that you trust their judgement.
- **Hold Them Accountable.** Remember that superior trust and subordinate autonomy is a two-way street. Holding employees accountable for their work and for meeting established goals and deadlines motivates them to achieve better results. Demand their best effort.
- **Provide Constructive Feedback.** Regardless of the results, let them know how they're doing, and give them the coaching they need to improve.

Although they might not always ask for it, they want and need your feedback to further develop their knowledge and skills.

- **Prompt Recognition Works Wonders.** Genuine one-on-one acknowledgement and recognition goes a long way toward reinforcing an employee's willingness to step up. Show you appreciate their above-and-beyond commitment with a reward. Often times, the best reward is additional trust and an added level of responsibility.
- **Allow People to Fail without Becoming Failures.** Exploit mistakes are a tool of progress.

If you want your men to take ownership in their jobs and work for you the way they'd work for themselves, you must invite them to be more than just an order-taking drone by cultivating a culture of autonomy—the DSOC.

Delegating ownership is important to stretch the subordinate leaders but it does not absolve the superior of the responsibility and accountability for the consequences and thus must remain engaged. A supportive leadership generates trust and promotes accountability.

Conclusion

Organisations that sustain success over a long time are based on values and a culture that keeps their people engaged. Engaged is distinctly different from committed. Engaged employees feel a sense of belonging and a sense of fulfilment.

Trust remains the key to engagement of the team and the onus lies on the leadership. A culture which accepts mistakes as a tool of learning and growth encourages innovation and exploitation of opportunities. This culture encourages the culture of taking of ownership. The culture of trust and ownership promotes development of leadership and generates momentum. An institutional and cultural practice of building leadership at all levels automatically promotes trust and ownership. Creating this environment is the responsibility of the leadership. The two go hand in hand.

Major General **Anil Sengar**, YSM, VSM (Retd), has vast operational experience having served both as an Infantry and a Mechanised Forces Officer. He commanded 5 GUARDS, a Rashtriya Rifles Sector in the Valley and a division in a Strike Corps. He was also the Deputy GOC of a division under raising in the North East. He has also served on a UN Mission in Cambodia and as Defence Attaché to Turkey, accredited to Syria and Lebanon. A prolific writer and a motivational speaker, he has written six books on a variety of subjects.

11

Need to Reinvigorate Leadership Training in Military Academies

Asit Mistry

"Give me a man or a woman with common sense and who is not an idiot and I assure you can make a leader out of him or her."

—Field Marshal Sam Manekshaw

Introduction

Leadership training imparted to young cadets at the Military Academies forms the bedrock of their future military careers. This very start and further grooming during their service have given rise to some of the greatest of military leaders of our times, who with their skills and leadership prowess have changed the very destiny of their countries. The training imparted to these young cadets, who are prospective leaders of men and women who would defend their nations in times to come, thus is very important. As is widely known "a living organism that does not grow is dead and what is dead will only decay". Therefore, there is a need to periodically re-examine the training being imparted at Military Academies, particularly the leadership training, take stock if it has kept up with the times and does it meet the present-day requirements and accordingly reinvigorate it as and when necessary. While the scope of training in military academies is very vast and all-encompassing, this article is restricted to the domain of leadership training being imparted in our military academies.

Two Models of Military Academies. There are essentially two models of military academies the world over; firstly, the **'West Point Model'** wherein young High School graduates undergo arduous military training, grooming and personality development along with academic education equivalent to University Graduation. The training duration is usually of three to four years. Besides US Military Academy, US Naval Academy, Japanese NDA and our own NDA, Indian Naval Academy (INA) as well as the Cadet Training Wings (CTW) of Indian Army follow this model. The second is the **'Sandhurst Model'** wherein the basic entry is university graduates. These academies, with much shorter training period that could range from 12 to 24 months, mainly focus on military leadership and tactical knowledge of warfighting at a Section/Platoon level. IMA, INA and AFA follow this model for Direct Entry candidates, as does the OTA, Chennai with slight modification.

Heritage. Our Pre-Commission Training Academies (PCTAs) have the great history and heritage of producing some of the finest leaders who have shaped the destiny of our country as well as the entire world. These PCTAs have produced officers who have led from the front and have been a breed apart. This includes most of the Service Chiefs, the first Field Marshal and the first CDS, besides such legendary heroes like Gurbachan Singh Salaria, Nirmaljeet Singh Sekhon, Arun Khetrapal, Manoj Pandey, Rakesh Sharma to name just a few. The leaders produced by our PCTAs have certainly lived up to the trust reposed in them by the Nation. It is that proud heritage and legacy that we all inherit. It is therefore the solemn duty of current leadership to ensure that our PCTAs and their training curriculum keep abreast with the changing times and shape leaders who shall carry the legacy through next 30-40 years, leaders who are capable of dealing with **future challenges and the changing nature of war.**

Critical Review. At the same time, we also need to critically examine if the Academies have kept up with the times, particularly in the domain of leadership training. While we do have inspiring examples of leadership by the officers trained in our Academies, there have been some prominent failures too, particularly some prominent cases of moral turpitude and rather mediocre performance, lack of critical thinking and obsessive conformity by a significant majority.

Future Warfare

Future wars would be radically different from the conventional wars that we are so used to. Wars are no longer merely geographical; they would be as much ideological. They would no longer be limited to territorial boundaries. Hybrid wars and grey zone actions are slowly overtaking the industrial age, conventional wars. Cutting-edge technology like AI, drones and cyberwarfare have irretrievably altered the way wars will be fought. Future conflicts would invariably be multispectral, multi-domain, decentralised and dispersed. They would be characterised by a compression of battle-space; compression of both the time and geographical dimensions. This also results in significant fusion of the three levels, levels, i.e., strategic, operational and tactical. What is purely a local, tactical issue can quickly spiral into a major politico-strategic dilemma and vice versa, calling for greater levels of maturity and understanding even at a relatively very junior level.

Disinformation, economic manipulation, proxies and insurgencies, diplomatic pressure, military actions as well as cyber-attacks, all or some of them, employed in an integrated manner would be the new norm. Quite often, such conflicts or confrontations may not cross the threshold of conventional war. The new forms of conflicts are more ambiguous in character and therefore designated as "grey zones". Adapting to such conflicts, which try to achieve political ends without transgressing into a traditional battlefield, where there could be more tactical transparency but greater strategic haze, is rather difficult and calls for **greater adaptability, versatility and flexibility among the future military leaders**. It calls for diverse and dynamic response, wherein leadership skills would be severely strained and challenged as never before in the past.

The challenges of modern conflicts are further compounded by the omnipresent, all-pervasive reach, speed and "in your face" repeats of **social media** which tend to give an exaggerated sense of reality. Information Warfare is now an integral element of all types of warfare. Our traditional methods and approach to leadership are very successful in churning out highly regimented, conformist leaders who can meet the requirements of centralised, hierarchical form of conventional warfare. However, are these training methods and approach adequate to meet the demands of future warfare? Isn't there a growing need to reinvigorate the military leadership training in PCTAs so as to create leaders who can meet the demands of a highly unpredictable, fluid and decentralised form of future military challenges? The future military leader needs to be a **scholar-soldier-diplomat**, all rolled into one comprehensive package as a multi-skilled expert who can handle weapons, technology as well as human resources; who has deep knowledge and understanding of complex issues, is flexible and dynamic enough to quickly adapt to the emerging situations.

Continuous Development. Future military leaders have to be trained and groomed physically, academically and morally at PCTAs to be able to meet the challenges of the future battlefield. While this unique conceptual mix of training has stood the test of time and has produced capable leaders ready to face older versions of predictable and linear challenges; the content, pedagogy, methods and training infrastructure of our PCTAs have to be continuously updated and reinvigorated. It must be reiterated that the training imparted at PCTAs is only foundational and basic. Therefore, it is equally important that the young leaders trained by these Academies learn to build upon their strong foundation during the course of their professional careers. Learning is a continuous and lifelong process. Learning is never complete and should never end.

The prospective leaders must realise that the standards set for themselves have to be much higher than what is expected out of their command. The troops that they would command in due course would be highly educated, tech savvy and rather adept at use of social media. They are even more aware than the troops of the past. Nothing can be hidden from them. Any lowering of standards would immediately diminish the respect they have for their leaders. The young leaders must be conscious that respect of their troops will have to be commanded, and not demanded.

Concept of Military Leadership for 21st Century

It is a universal maxim that leaders are not born, but made. That is the cardinal principle of training in PCTAs. Therefore, leadership requires hard work, dedication and sincerity. It means developing professional knowledge and competence, it means knowing the troops and understanding their needs. It means empathy for their command and the ability to reach out and communicate with them. Leadership implies initiative, which in turn implies, not to await orders but anticipate them and take appropriate action; and in the absence of orders, assume them and take action. The PCTAs therefore need to inculcate such initiative rather than kill it which is typically symbolised by the old adage of "young leaders are not be heard but only seen" or "who told you to think?" and so on.

The legendary **"Charge of the Light Brigade"**, so beautifully immortalised by the inspiring poem of Lord Alfred Tennyson, particularly its most famous catchphrase, **"Yours not to reason why but to do or die"** has been the epitome of military values and leadership in the 19th and 20th centuries. However, that approach would not take us very far in the 21st century. Instead, it must be reconfigured to say *"Yours is but to reason how & why, and YET to do or die"*. The cadets have to be trained to be leaders of combatants. Leadership is not a matter of ordering around subordinates or juniors. The ability as a leader does not depend on rank but the ability to influence the command through actions. It is the initiative that one takes, the examples that he/she sets and the influence that it generates is what makes an effective leader.

Influence comes through example. Leading by example is the touchstone of leadership. Setting an example in everything, small or big—be it turnout, punctuality, sense of cleanliness and hygiene, management of time, even financial propriety and so on. Leadership means assuming responsibility and taking ownership. A military leader can never take shelter behind past precedents, SOPs or this common refrain "but sir, this is how it has always been done". While all these should certainly guide the young leaders, they cannot be the 'be all and end all' of everything. Once a military leader is on the scene, the responsibility of doing anything—whatever task it may be—rests squarely on their shoulders. Therefore, they should have the courage of conviction to bring in appropriate course correction should they disagree with the precedent or the SOP. Being mindful of the circumstances or the environment since the time the SOP was made may have changed completely. So an SOP or accepted/established norm of doing things cannot give leaders a licence not to apply their own minds, re-examine it and make suitable changes—albeit with due approval of the appropriate authority, as the case may be. It is this kind of responsible and responsive leadership that our PCTAs need to inculcate rather than the traditional approach of 'never volunteer'.

Leaders need to be trained to bring in changes so as to make their group more effective, more efficient and more cohesive. As a corollary, change management is one of the cardinal functions of leadership. Leadership also means the moral courage to enforce the right standards, to point out a mistake or to own up to one and to correct a wrong, not shying away from calling a spade a spade. Equally, they should never expect the troops to do what they themselves are not prepared to do. The ultimate hallmark of a leader continues be someone who says "FOLLOW ME" rather than "GO ON".

Morals and Ethics. A crucial element of leadership training in PCTAs that needs a relook is inculcating right values among cadets vis-à-vis upholding 'traditions'. The latter usually have a logical origin, more often than not to enhance organisational efficiency and/or effectiveness. Over a period of time, they may lose relevance but gather a life of their own. Traditions that become irrelevant and/or retard organisational growth must be jettisoned. Traditions must always be dynamic and adoptive. Unfortunately, a lot of gibberish is pursued in the garb of 'traditions', misplaced sense of 'smartness' or the so-called ability to 'manage'. Sometimes an operational veneer too is given to justify such malpractices. Using guile or deception in operations is not synonymous with cheating in exams or lying to cover up an offence. As against dynamic traditions, values remain eternal. There is no substitute for imparting right moral values to the young leaders. There are numerous steps already incorporated in the academies by way of Honour Code, Dos and Don'ts, Academy Prayer and so on. Unfortunately their implementation or adherence tends to get eroded over time and that needs to be guarded against. In this context it also needs to be realised that not all the moral failures displayed by officers in the course of their careers should be blamed on the training, or the lack of it, at the PCTAs. Moral fibre is as much a product of the foundation training as the influence of the environment through which an individual has grown and evolved. Thus the value system adopted in the Services in the units, formations and establishments, where the officers serve for long years, play much greater role in the orientation of their moral compasses.

Creative Thinking, Decisiveness and Initiative. Deliberate and structured training is essential to impart skills of creative thinking, to 'think outside the box' so to say and come up with innovative solutions, that too on the basis of incomplete information. We also have to break the mould of "conforming" which tends to produce templated solutions and apprehension of standing apart from the crowd. We also need to train new generation leaders to be decisive, exercise initiative, assume responsibility and take ownership. Unfortunately, we tend to treat "initiative" and "decision-making" as sources of electricity—to be turned on only under certain situations and then to be disconnected the moment circumstances change. Unfortunately, we only promote insecurity and inculcate timidity among young leaders by such an approach. Therefore, cadets (and young officers) have to be encouraged to voice their views fearlessly, follow their conscience and take decisions. Having done so, we need to stand by them so that they are reassured and gain confidence in decision-making rather than looking over their shoulders.

Team Spirit. Another important aspect that PCTAs excel in inculcating is Team Spirit. However, this too warrants some course correction. The much-touted Course Spirit or Squadron Spirit forms the foundation of the lessons of Team Spirit. A simple definition of a Team is, One for All and All for One. For a soldier, the Team is always more important than his own self. Sporting legend, Michael Jordan has said, "Talent Wins Games, but Team Work and Intelligence Wins Championships". For leaders who want to achieve something substantial in life—and not just some momentary success in one odd game, but want to excel in the championship of life—there is no substitute for Team Work. Essentially, in battle, you cannot leave a man behind. More important, the team must believe that no one would be left behind under a leader's watch—the sky would be the limit for a young leader who can create that feeling among his team. **However, covering up a wrong done by a mate or using unethical means to win some championship is not Team Spirit.** It would certainly not help us win battles. It may momentarily help a colleague but would not make him a strong leader and may actually endanger the lives of troops that the weak leader may ultimately command. **Such misplaced sense of Team Spirit has to be discouraged.**

Discipline. Future leaders must be encouraged to make discipline their way of life. It has to become lifestyle. Discipline is what differentiates an armed force from a crowd. Discipline is 'the soul of the army' as George Washington put it. There is nothing new about the importance of discipline. What has to change is the attitude and approach. Enforced Discipline has to be replaced by **"Self-Discipline"**—which is an imperative of the decentralised, modern battle field. Self-discipline begins with the individual, and encompasses the whole—the body, mind and soul of the individual and should extend to the entire team. It demands fitness, obedience, cleanliness, orderliness and time management;

of which punctuality is merely the first step. The most important aspect of self-discipline is moral. **Truth** and **selflessness** which form part of the Honour Code of most Academies have to be the cornerstones of this moral sense. The courage to do what is right, sometimes even against the majority view of colleagues and at times even orders of the superiors, requires moral conviction.

Physical Fitness. Young officers ought to continue to focus on physical fitness, their own as well as of their command. Ultimately, in all forms of warfare and irrespective of the level of technology or the type of platform one uses, combat demands not only great skill but the ultimate level of fitness, endurance and persistence. Joe Henderson, an American Footballer says, "Your **toughness** is made up of equal parts of **persistence** and **experience**. You do not so much outrun your opponents as **outlast** and **outsmart** them. And the **toughest opponent** of all is the one **inside your head**." Therefore, if leaders are determined to achieve something, they have to be at it with diligence, persistence, patience and single-minded dedication. PCTAs must encourage young leaders to start enjoying physical activity and follow a lifelong quest for physical fitness. The approach has to be scientific, creative and holistic.

Reading. The importance of reading and widening professional horizon for military leaders cannot be overemphasised. It is a challenge to inculcate the reading habit among youngsters whose attention span is so easily undermined with smartphones and entertainment platforms. Gen James Mattis, the former US Defence Secretary emphasised the importance of reading for a military leader by saying that—either you learn through the experience of others or you learn the hard way—the experience at the cost of lives of men you command. Therefore, there is no substitute for reading and widening the horizon of young leaders.

Transformation of Instructions Staff. To achieve these fundamental changes and course correction in leadership training in PCTAs, a major transformation would be required among the trainers themselves, i.e., the Instructional Staff popularly called the Directing Staff (DS), particularly the young Divisional Officers/Platoon Commanders and their equivalents. Unfortunately, instead of being the harbingers of change, they tend to act like 7th/8th termers or 'super appointments'. Their 'my time' syndrome is far stronger than those with more experience and maturity; and therefore most reluctant to change. Accordingly, the first major step has to bring about significant changes, rather a transformation among the instructors of our PCTAs, particularly among the largest and the most proximate element. This would then pave the way for further changes and reinvigoration of leadership training in our PCTAs. Even for selection of instructors for PCTAs too, a revised approach is warranted. The elements of 'maturity, understanding and empathy' need to be given as much importance as course grading, annual appraisals and other conventional parameters of judging professional competence and instructional potential.

Conclusion

Leaders of our Armed Forces have more than proved their mettle. Their professionalism, sacrifice, courage and commitment have earned unparalleled trust of the entire nation for the Armed Forces. We cannot afford to undermine this sacred trust. We have to make appropriate adjustments in our training curriculum to meet the demands of the modern battlefield and changing nature of warfare as also factor in the imperatives of the changing sociocultural milieu of our society (and therefore of our intake), and despite these complex challenges shape the most competent, capable and dedicated leadership that is worthy of our armed forces and thereby retain the cutting edge that our profession demands.

The Armed Forces are at the crossroads to adopt to the rapid changes in warfare, technology and increasingly complex nature of threats to national security. While the increasingly short lifespan of technology has its own challenges, keeping our human resources battleworthy in this milieu remains the most critical responsibility of the military leadership. Reaffirming the primacy of the "Honour Code" to build strong foundations of ethical values and integrity have become an even more indispensable part of training in our Academies. It is equally significant that our academies equip our future leaders to be SCHOLAR-SOLDIERS-CUM-DIPLOMATS who can operate in the technologically intense battlefield environment characterised by ever-increasing complexities and ambiguities. The leadership training in our Academies must be reoriented so as to retain our edge despite these challenges.

Lieutenant General **Asit Mistry**, PVSM, AVSM, SM, VSM (Retd), superannuated from service on November 1, 2021. His last assignment, prior to his superannuation, was as the Commandant, National Defence Academy, Khadakwasla. Prior to that, he was GOC Delhi Area. He has also been the Colonel of the MARATHA LI. He is a graduate of Defence Services Staff College and Higher Command Course. He has commanded an infantry battalion in Siachen Glacier, a Mountain Brigade in Upper Assam and a Rashtriya Rifles Force in Kashmir. He is currently Director, School of Internal Security, Defence and Strategic Studies (SISDSS) at Rashtriya Raksha University (RRU), Gandhinagar (Gujarat).

12

Team of Teams

Synergising Efforts of Small Teams

Yash Mor

"None of us is as smart as all of us."

—Ken Blanchard

The future battle-space is going to be complicated with information overload and domination of technology. The leaders on top of any organisational structure are going to be grappling with a host of multidimensional agencies involved in the conduct of operations or in support. Many of these organisations or agencies may not even understand the rank structure and hierarchy of a traditional military organisation.

The demands on the leadership in conventional operations or Counter Insurgency, will be high to achieve goals and objectives. The mission will be achieved only with close coordination of many agencies and organisations. The military leaders will have to show team building skills to enhance not only the potential of our own teams but also incorporate many others in a manner that everyone feels part of the vision of the leader and contributes to the attainment of the goals and objectives.

For the armed forces, it is only a matter of time before the Tri-service nature with integrated theatre commands takes shape. The ability to take the other service along and exploiting their full potential will depend on the understanding of joint operations. While each service will be part of the mission, however, success will greatly depend on the ability of the senior leadership to create a mutually benefiting 'team spirit'. While this is possible due to our years of joint training the real challenge will be to take on board many government agencies including Police and Intelligence agencies. Thus, leadership competence to handle disparate organisations may be the key to success.

In an organisation like the Army, with clearly defined protocols and hierarchy, passing of orders and execution takes place almost automatically. There are very few avenues left for the subordinates to give a feedback or suggest any better manner of task accomplishment. This does work fine till the time the situation escalates into a crisis. Invariably the leaders get little or no feedback from lower headquarters of the 'quality' or implementability of the order. We have had numerous instances where Team Spirit and a sense of being part of decision-making could have averted many unfortunate episodes. The recent clashes with China in Eastern Ladakh resulted in the death of over 20 brave men, including a Commanding Officer and grievous injuries to many may have been avoided if the entire military leadership had been in communication in the nature of a team of teams. A lot of the instructions and orders passed through the many echelons of intermediate staff are more often than not subjected to distortion and noise. The 'spirit' of a decision may not reach the intended audience.

The Kargil conflict erupted when the Pakistani intruders were located in multiple locations over a frontage of almost 160 km. The headquarters responsible for the surveillance of the area was quite oblivious of the developing situation over an entire season. In many such instances direct communication with a large number of teams spread across a large frontier could have been networked onto a common platform. It is quite obvious that a 'Team of Teams' created within the overall military concept of Mission Orders or Directive Style of Command will not only save lives but also empower leadership at various levels to take positive actions based on the shared vision.

Balancing Leadership and Teamwork

While a lot depends on the leadership style of the senior leader, a few best practices which can be inculcated very early in the career of officers may be good tools in balancing leadership requirements and team formation. The habit of making effective teams starts early in the career of any officer and stays long after superannuation. As a young officer it's the ability to make your sub-unit not only fighting fit but also a team with a high state of morale and motivation. Later this ability continues in senior ranks where this can be a battle-winning factor.

- **Vision and proactive.** The leaders need to have a clear vision for the team and should be able to convey the same. The responsibility of the leader on top is to be always proactive so that the integration of new members in the team is seamless and smooth.
- **Trust building and integrity of thought.** The key to success of teams depends to a great extent on the ability of the senior leadership to build trust. Trust along with integrity of thought is of utmost importance, specially for those who are part of a mission and do not form part of the integral organisation structure.
- **Communication.** The ability of the commander to communicate effectively with each team is crucial at each stage. Before communicating the leader needs to develop an intrinsic ability to listen. These days technology allows leaders to effectively communicate with teams that may not even be co-located. The leaders should not shy away from using all media available to directly communicate with each sub-part of the team. Time wasters like structured conferences must be avoided as they seldom give any dividends compared to the time wasted.
- **Personal rapport.** Every effort must be made to establish a personal rapport with each element of the team. All avenues available to establish such a rapport must be utilised. In a crisis the personal touch and familiarity solve complex problems as compared to official communications.
- **Collaborate with a Win-Win attitude.** It's essential that each team feels they are contributing to the overall success of the mission. The necessity to collaborate from a habit of win-win is essential to get the willing participation of all the echelons of the teams.
- **Creativity and unconventional approach.** The leader needs to generate a lot of creative ideas from the interaction with the teams. The ability to listen, thus is of paramount importance, more often than not in the army, the senior appears to be 'know all', very seldom do officers generate creative and unconventional ideas. This is again to be cultivated at a much younger service bracket, or else it's too late and we have a lot of "yes, siring" all around.

- **Objective orientation of the leaders and the teams.** The entire focus of the leaders and members of the team should be focused towards the attainment of the goal. Above all the leader should appear to be beyond personal glory in the mission. In peacetime, we do have selfish leaders walk away with all accolades and distinguished awards. However, this trend is likely to result in disaster in case of a large-scale war in the future.

Examples of Team Building

From the Diary of a Company Commander in Counter-Insurgency. A tenure in the Rashtriya Rifles (RR) as a very senior company commander was the first real test of making teams out of disparate organisations. Many of them at times working at cross-purposes or at best in their own organisational or personal interest. Leading a Company in South Kashmir (Anantnag District) was a challenge since a large number of army units, paramilitary, intelligence agencies, state police, development agencies, NGOs, etc., worked in the area extending from Anantnag town onwards to the Pir Panjal ranges, popularly known as the Bringhi river valley and the Gadhol Valley. The company itself was located almost 30 km from the battalion Headquarters, with one platoon of the company a further 20 km away. The company was housed inside a burnt down (almost completely destroyed in a fire by the terrorists in the early part of the insurgency in 1990) tourist resort of Kokernag. Alongside this was also the battalion headquarters and other elements of a BSF unit. Opposite across the road was a Police station. Near the police station was a post of CRPF. Inside the company bunkers was a small prefabricated shelter with a detachment of Intelligence Bureau. Very frequently a Team of Para SF troops was deployed in the company area of responsibility (AOR). To add to the plethora of forces many times the Naval Marine Commandos (MARCOS) too would be in the area for a sizeable period of time.

In a scenario like this, the choice was to do routine activities or try something different. While I was picking up the nuances of operating in a dense insurgency environment, an effort was made to touch base with all the disparate organisations and agencies. Initially the response was at best cold or indifferent. However persistent contact at personal levels ironed out many issues of mutual faith and trust. The small IB det of three people became my eyes and ears, a lot of intelligence was corroborated with them. We supported each other and became closely linked in sharing information real time. We were successful in breaking many barriers, the result was that the information which we would have got after a few days filtered down from our senior headquarters was with me even before it reached higher up. With the SF, we established a direct connect and helped each other numerous times without higher headquarters even knowing about it. The J&K police from the SHO and *munshi* of the thana to the SP of the district were on the same wavelength.

With the BSF and CRPF again we established a very cordial and mutually respecting attitude. Since we lived in and around the same complex, we avoided one-upmanship and openly shared best practices. Often at very short notice we supported each other with troops and administrative requirements. The team spirit galvanised the entire security forces under an overall objective of eliminating top leadership of all the active terror groups. At the same time, we established a redressal mechanism to help the local populace in times of need as also winning hearts and minds. In a synergised effort together all the forces succeed in killing over 200 hard core terrorists in 2001-2003. With zero cases of human rights violations and a conduct of a very successful assembly elections in October 2002. The spirit had a downward trickle effect such that junior leadership of all the organisations too got into the act and were more than willing to put in that extra effort when needed.

COVID and the Handling of Iran Evacuees. In April 2020, the nation was grappling with the pandemic and the forces were required to create facilities for quarantine of Indians returning from foreign countries. No one seemed to have all the answers to this new form of virus. The nature of the disease and its spread was still unknown and almost everyone was groping in the dark. During this situation we were given the responsibility to receive and house our citizens being evacuated from Iran. This was an operation we were least trained for. It involved a huge logistics and medical exercise.

The number of organisations that were directly involved in bringing the Indian citizens ranged from Air India, our Embassy in Tehran, office of CDS, Ministry of Defence, Ministry of External Affairs, Army Headquarters (military operations and logistics groups), Indian Air Force, Civil Administration in Jodhpur, Police and Health services of the state of Rajasthan. Later the Civil

Administration of J&K and Ladakh too came in the picture since almost all evacuees belonged to these two Union Territories.

While preparing to house over 1,100 people in Jaisalmer and Jodhpur, the Corps Headquarters was dealing with a large number of completely incongruent organisations. The first step was to establish a COVID Empowerment Committee under the Chief of Staff. The committee started the process of integrating all the different organisations and established direct linkages with the personalities involved in this complicated exercise.

The net result was that these evacuees from Iran stayed in the army camp for over two months without even one fatal case. We had senior citizens who were in Iran for pilgrimage from Kashmir and Ladakh. We also had a large contingent of Indian students studying medicine in Iran, most of the people were from Kargil and Kashmir. Once they were all cleared of coronavirus, we had to start sending them back home, this was again a massive logistics nightmare.

The entire Operation NAMASTE was a huge morale booster and a success because we were able to form a Team Spirit among all those who were involved. The use of technology for reaching out to people breaking the laid down protocols of seniority and status helped in ensuring that we achieved our common objective of taking care of our own citizens stuck in a foreign country, and most of them having tested positive were also needing psychological counselling. The entire operation gave an immense sense of joy when all people returned to their homes in Kargil and Kashmir valley, many of them openly saying that they have a high regard for the Indian army and its ethos.

The two examples above indicate one common factor, that is the **ability of the leader to see beyond himself.** This is the mantra for forming successful teams in all kinds of scenarios and situations. It is also an attempt at **distributed leadership**, allowing to tap into every pocket of wisdom and advice that exists within the team. The officials handling health services at Jodhpur were frequently called upon on web-based links to give timely advice and suggestions on handling old citizens. The leadership at Ladakh, including the Member of Parliament, were frequently in touch to convey the well-being of the people in our facilities. They formed an essential bridge between the evacuees and their families back in the villages.

Characteristics of Effective Teams

It is essential to know the basic characteristics of effective teams, this would come in handy for team leaders as well as the members in building common blocks for transformation of successful teams.

- **Mutual Trust.** The entire success of the team depends on mutual trust and faith. In fact, building trust and then jealously guarding it, is essential for successful and effective teams. The trust levels should be so high that each member can predict what the other will do.
- **Mission Oriented.** The team must be always focused on the mission accomplishment. All members and sub-teams must have the ability to work together to accomplish the mission.
- **Adaptable.** The team must be adaptable to change its course with the challenges that may be demanding, specially in active operational and insurgency affected areas. Flexibility in mind and actions is needed not only at the top but at all echelons of the team. Many times, a setback throws the team off-gear leading to despondency and the futility of continuing with the mission. At such times the leaders need to step forward not only to recalibrate opinions but also reorientate towards the objectives.
- **Execution of tasks and Sense of Responsibility.** The success of the teams depends to a great extent on the manner of execution of tasks and deep sense of responsibility among all the members. The spirit should be to support each other and provide whatever positive strokes in fulfilling the tasks. In fact, the effort should be to not only meet but, if possible, exceed the expected standards.
- **Pride in Accomplishments.** The sense of accomplishment is necessary for teams to continue to pursue overall objectives. The leaders must ensure that credits and awards are shared in a transparent manner. A true leader will always put the interests of his subordinates in honours and awards. Many senior officers walk away with awards almost every year in senior ranks much to the dislike of the teams they were leading. Medal **'infection'** continues unabated. The race for distinguished awards among the senior officers is largely now on epidemic scale. On the contrary, great leaders actually avoid self-gratification at all costs.
- **Internal Team vs External Team.** It is very easy to motivate and inspire the internal team, that is direct under command, since they are in the reporting

channel of the top leadership; however the challenge for military leaders is to get the same kind of response from external teams. These consist of attachments from outside the formation, other services, police, civil government, contractors, civil society leaders and political representatives. At no cost should a stage be reached that it becomes internal versus external, such a situation can quickly spiral into a distrust. At all times it's the prime responsibility of the leader and his staff to keep the external team involved and informed.

Building Trust: Most Important Leadership Challenge

One of the basic foundations of any successful team is to build trust and mutual faith amongst all the team members. The onus for this lies squarely on the senior leadership. Long peace tenures create a sense of 'all is well' since the test of trust is in actual combat when the situation becomes critical and life threatening. Trust survives when the level of integrity and personal dependability of senior leadership is unquestionable. This allows subordinates to concentrate all their energies in performance of task at hand. People are prepared to put their own life in danger when they have implicit faith and trust in the team leaders. Some of the practices which help create an atmosphere of trust are:

- The senior leaders must very often express mutual trust in the team. He should make use of numerous opportunities to directly communicate with each member, if possible.
- A lot of opportunities must be provided for social interaction. The smaller teams need to meet other teams as often as possible, technology must be exploited if needed for the same.
- A system of regular feedback to team members is a must. The communication must be two ways.
- In the initial days, it is important to build trust by increasing transparency and accessibility of senior leadership. In our feudal culture the senior leadership are hardly accessible to rank and file. A few measures like removing the culture of 'red lights' must be done away with. Too many soldiers on duty guarding senior leadership needs to be avoided.
- It may happen that a few issues of mistrust crop up in large teams. Quick efforts must be taken to **mitigate distrust.** Be fair and open about issues

that may cause distrust. Share rewards and success equally across the team members.

- Team leader needs to be a very **effective listener**, this is a quality severely lacking in our senior leadership. Encourage brainstorming and open-house sessions with free flow of ideas. These help in fostering teamwork, cohesion and cooperation.

Exploit all Avenues of Interaction. Work is done in two settings: formal and informal; high-performance teams must master both. While using formal occasions to impress upon goals and objectives related to mission accomplishment, the informal forums are great for situational awareness and build camaraderie among team members. The value of the formal interactions is enhanced if the informal channel is fully functional and not caught up in the steep ladder of ranks and appointments. Unfortunately many informal events are turning out to be very strict on protocols and thus a wonderful opportunity to meet people is lost.

OODA Loop. The team that can **observe, orient, decide, and act faster** will be always ahead of the competition. The senior leadership must remain proactive to anticipate future course of actions, this habit can initiate faster OODA cycle. The objective is to build teams that can "connect the dots" ahead of others to influence outcomes across the entire spectrum of operations.

The team's success is interdependent, not independent. The defence forces rely on effective teams to complete tasks, achieve objectives, and accomplish missions. The nation looks at our armed forces as the last bastion of national integration and they are always expected to accomplish all missions without fail. The ability to build teams through mutual trust and maintain effective, cohesive teams throughout military operations is an essential skill for senior commanders, staff officers and junior leaders. The diversity and size of a team, nature and structure of the team will keep changing but the challenge for the leaders is always to maintain effective teams.

Teams are an essential part of the Indian Army. At a very young service many junior leaders learn to operate outside the comfort zones of their units. They have to be given challenging assignments where the nuances of team building can be learnt, middle-level leaders must mentor young officers so that they in future turn out to be genuine military leaders and not 'climbers'. To get the most out of any team, the team must be cohesive and effective, which does not just happen by chance. It takes hard work, time and immense qualities of leadership to develop a team. Once the team achieves a high level of cohesion, it is critical to sustain it at that level till the end of the mission or tenure of the team.

13

Professional Military Education in the Armed Forces

AB Shivane

Abstract

Professional Military Education (PME) is the ultimate high ground on which we create and nurture inquisitive, thoughtful and confident leaders to "Think, Fight and Win" future conflicts. The three elements of intellectual capital that link military education to military effectiveness are stable civil-military fusion, a culture of reflection and capacity for critical thinking.

The need is to review, refine and strengthen Professional Military Education (PME) objectives, curriculum and institutions to develop agile and adaptive future leaders with optimal competence in the art and science of warfare, to achieve intellectual overmatch beyond just hardware. Thus training for certainty and educating for uncertainty are two sides of the same coin and need an optimal balance.

The current training philosophy, joint training doctrine and biennial training directives while comprehensive are doctrinally oriented to fight the last war in the conventional domain with mention of grey zone, disruptive technologies and multi-domain warfare more as a realisation than manifestation. The article proposes a PME policy with concrete recommendations for desired outcomes.

War, Warfare and PME Construct

Defence Forces across the world are witnessing a paradigm shift in the character of war and conduct of warfare. The transformation in the character of warfare has impacted the physical, cognitive and moral dimensions beyond just the military. The very definition of war and peace has undergone a fundamental change. There is a definitive shift from the kinetic domain to the cognitive domain in which victory or defeat is defined by the triumph of narratives. This has brought about a paradigm shift in why, where, how and with what wars will be fought. Thus the creative application of military power, integrating all instruments of national power, and adapting to conditions of disruptive change in a peace-war continuum is imperative. In this complex security environment, uniformed leaders will have to step out of their silos to shape and influence the battle-space with a greater ascent in the cognitive domain. The defence forces will accordingly need to review their objectives and structures in the identification, education, preparation and development of future leaders.

PME must develop warriors, with both cognitive and warfighting capabilities, seamlessly fusing training and education, and linking it to military effectiveness in the future battle-space. *The three elements of intellectual capital that link military education to military effectiveness are stable civil-military fusion, a culture of reflection and capacity for critical thinking.* All these require greater investment in the Indian context. The aim should be to develop strategically-minded joint warfighters who are skilled in both the science and art of war. PME must not only make leaders more creative and less risk-averse but practise the skill of critical thought. As the Indian Defence Forces undertake transformation, challenged by fiscal austerity, ascending multi-domain threats and skewed intellectual capital, empowered PME must be a foundational construct for leaders of tomorrow.

The PME Need

The need is to review, refine and strengthen PME objectives, curriculum and institutions to develop agile and adaptive future leaders with optimal competence in the art and science of warfare, to achieve intellectual overmatch beyond just hardware.

Intellectual Overmatch in Battle-space

Intellectual overmatch and mental agility are created by a balanced continuum of training, education, experience. Training to fight and educating to fight and win the war, are mutually complementary yet distinct in their domains. Training is essentially skilling and teaches "muscle memory" in the kinetic energy domain. Education is the knowledge that harnesses "intellectual memory" and is in the potential energy domain. Training teaches a person what to do, whereas education teaches a person how to think. Education facilitates reasoning ability, which, in turn, is critical in responding to disruptive changes. Thus, *training for certainty and educating for uncertainty are two sides of the same coin and need an optimal balance.* This is crucial to leaders at all levels. It encompasses a range of disciplines centred around developing strategically minded, critically-thinking, and creative joint warfighters skilled in the art of war and the science of the application of lethal military power. This will be the foundational construct in which future leaders will think innovatively and achieve intellectual overmatch to outmanoeuvre, out-think and out-innovate adversaries, to sustain a competitive advantage beyond just hardware. This requires a learning continuum and career-long professional development ethos focused on cognitive capabilities and not the present episodic educational opportunities, which are neither attuned nor adaptive to meet future challenges. It must never be forgotten that the *potential energy of the cognitive domain is the primary driver for the kinetic energy of the bullet.*

Creativity and Critical Thinking as a Military Culture

The military as a profession of arms is unique in many ways. It owes allegiance to the constitution for selfless service to the nation, extending to the risk of life itself. Its culture is embedded in the intellectual, professional and traditional values of the organisation. Yet it is confined by rules and regulations and pyramidical progression often defined by institutional authoritarianism and bureaucratic assessment. Thus, organisationally military breeds a leader who is conformist and more often than not subdues those who are reformist.

Conformism is a retarder to creativity in individuals and group consensus the antithesis of critical thinking. Thus while conformity breeds peacetime progression, creativity in war gets compromised. Military establishments that sponsor conformity in peacetime are doomed to stagnate and eventually fail in war. A creative approach emphasises the idea of seeing, thinking and exploring something new and not relying on the cut, copy, paste syndrome or the "pinks". It thus has *two elements of thinking, one which is reproductive and the second which is productive thinking.* Reproductive thinking is seeking past solutions to solve a present problem similar to one encountered in the past. This type of thinking leads to doctrinal conformist problem solving by the manual and leads to refighting the last battle. By contrast, productive thinking seeks a novel search for solutions based on different perspectives yet sound in military logic which is not only workable but has higher chances of success.

So how does a military organisation develop creativity and critical thinking skills? It is imperative to make critical thinking skills alongside military reasoning as assessment in the PME programme and career progression. It must be stated as a starred attribute. The critical thinker qualities must reflect on a leader's creative traits of being inquisitive, well-informed, seeking military reasoning, open-minded, flexible, accepting constructive criticism, prudent in making judgments, and seeking a fresh perspective in problem-solving.

Strategic Thinking for Military Leaders

As the character of wars undergoes a paradigm shift, so also the three hierarchical levels of tactical, operational and strategic domains, often displayed as a pyramid, now exhibit increasing fluidity and interaction as explained in Michael Handel's model of interaction below.

Figure 13.1: Michael Handel's Complex Model of Interaction

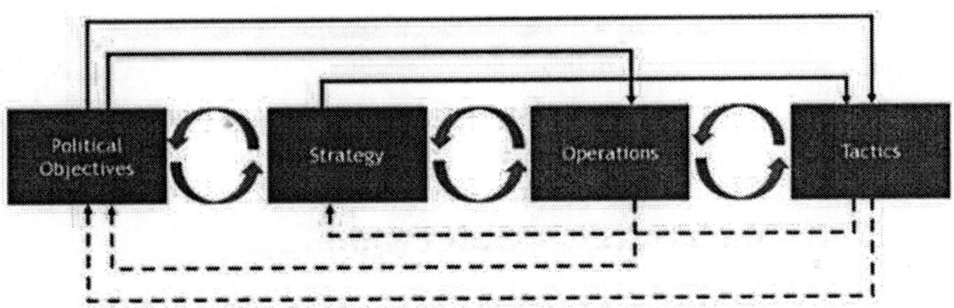

Strategic thinking competence must thus find space at all levels starting with awareness at the junior level to the application at the senior level. Increasingly, in the digital information age, tactical actions have a strategic effect as witnessed in the recent past both at Galwan and in the Nagaland ambush incidents. Leaders will have to deal with an entirely new set of intellectual, cultural and strategic challenges that were not present even a decade ago.

The larger picture defines victory not by force on force but by removing all options of the adversary and creating multi-domain dilemmas in a concerted manner to sap his will. Thus, understanding war and strategy is an attribute for all warfighters to target the will. Further, it must be remembered that strategy is performance and performance requires practice. Curricula in PME must accordingly include strategy development and students must learn the art of ends, ways and means as part of their research and war games to develop a perspective on macro issues. A failure to understand a military problem in the overall perspective of socio-political, economic, technological, cultural, ethical, and lethal complexity can be a disaster recipe for the nation.

Technology and Leader Fusion

The technological revolution of the 21st century is only likely to intensify in future. Possibly the most disruptive changes have been driven by the emergent technology and revolution in military affairs signalling the rise of a military-techno culture in which time, space, force and information dimensions have radically changed. Technology, particularly autonomous systems, information warfare and artificial intelligence, has changed the character of strategic leadership and smart warfighting. Yet the most critical and central factor will remain the man behind the machine. *The imperative is for adaptive leadership to emergent technology, which is knowledge-based, decision-oriented and optimises joint force capability*. Yet the critical challenge defence forces face is not how emergent technology will deliver outcomes, but rather it is reshaping of military bureaucracies and higher leadership culturally, that will shape the way we understand, adapt, integrate and exploit technology.

Adaptability is more in the cognitive quality and cannot be guaranteed by technology. This would require management of change of how we train to fight and how we fight to win in a digital era. Management of change requires primacy of cultural acceptance. Culture is an enduring phenomenon that always pays a price for technology unless the culture is evolutionary and mindsets agile. Strategic leaders must thus learn to harness the positive dimensions of culture to reorient it to the realities of changes driven by technology.

Thus, future leadership in the information and digital age will need to be trained through innovative instructional delivery means across a range of disciplines centred around technology interface and simulations. This will require a greater fusion between education and training and an optimal blend of the art and science of warfare. Art is to visualise, describe, direct, and lead, and science is to adapt, exploit and optimise the technology. Presently there is a sub-optimal blend of the science of warfare. Lack of this facet leads to technophobia, and resistance to technology adaption which is critical for future warfighting.

PME Attributes for Future Military Leaders

> *"The most important tool that any soldier carries is not his weapon, but his mind."*
>
> —General David H. Petraeus

The distinction between a good and a great leader will magnify in effect in the future battle-space of multi-domain warfare with overlapping needs of a scholar and a warrior. Thus, to cultivate future military leaders through the medium of PME, leadership attributes need to balance skills, knowledge and experience. The mechanism to quantify and evaluate them without hampering the learning curve remains the primary challenge. Some of these leadership attributes that PME must focus on are as follows:

(a) Ability to comprehend the larger strategic picture of the security environment and military as an integrated instrument of national power.

(b) Comprehend and adapt to the paradigm shifts in warfare, to reorient leaders, structures and doctrines for future warfighting, with an ascent on indigenous character.

(c) Ability to work through the blurred line between risk and danger and retain composure to surprise and ambiguity.

(d) Develop offensive spirit and proactive mindsets working from the hope of success rather than fear of failure.

(e) Possess the *revised 5Cs—Competence* (multi-domain with technology interface), *Character* (based on values and service ethics), *Critical thinking* (leading to creativity), *Cultural agility* (for transformation and change management), and *Communication skill* (extending from strategic to tactical level).

(f) Agility to manage change before change manages them and bring in the doctrinal transformation of cultures, structures and force application by leading the transition.

(g) Leaders must be seen, heard and have the power to communicate with capability and credibility in an environment wherein the notion of victory is all about narratives and perceptions.

(h) Comprehend, adapt and exploit the technology revolution and interface it to optimise the effects in the battle-space.

Current PME Challenges in the Indian Defence Forces

Combat as an instrument of warfare must relate to war as an instrument of politics and PME as a means to bridge the two. *The present system is mired by bureaucratic red tape, silo-based culture and standard curriculum which is essentially a wash, rinse and repeat narrative.* Inspiring a culture of transformation in PME requires more than service-designed laboratories and investing in greater intellectual capital beyond the uniform. The challenge is how, and to what end?

The current training philosophy, joint training doctrine and biennial training directives while comprehensive are *doctrinally oriented to fight the last war in the conventional domain with mention of grey zone, disruptive technologies and multi-domain warfare more as a realisation than manifestation.* Thus conceptually its transition to PME objectives and institutions has not manifested in keeping with future conflicts. Institutional integrated joint training is more symbolic and lacks cross-pollination and joint billeting at the cutting edge. PME remains focused more on training than balancing it with education and lacks institutional integration with strategy, technology and cross-domain learning. The structures too remain archival embedded in the Peace Establishment mental blocks of yesteryear. There are far too many overlapping headquarters overseeing training in silos both inter- and intra-service, rather than its synergisation under a single Joint Training Command. Instructor student mentoring takes precedence over instructor-student partnering to generate novel solutions to complex problems. There is limited space for promoting out of box ideas and creating incubator spaces to link ideas to an outcome. Training the trainers for institutionalised responsibilities is another neglected aspect mostly relying on the course grading premise which may have become archival. Selection of best trainers and their continuity remains a career management challenge, so "you reap what you sow". There is also a limited culture of cross-domain interface and learning between uniformed and non-uniformed fraternity who may otherwise be a part of the overall defence ecosystem. The distance education programmes too have yet to strike the right cultural chord and impact. Further, there is inadequate thought and investment in PME of JCOs/Senior NCOs in keeping with the present operational dynamics.

Thus, the current PME is neither attuned to present realities nor adaptive to future challenges. *PME has become a means for careerism rather than intellectual empowerment, thereby proverbially missing the woods for the trees.* Its pyramidal progression further inhibits lateral empowerment and fosters "doing well" to reach the next milestone irrespective of the means. Ambition to reach higher ranks in a pyramidical structure has often resulted in bottling up creative thoughts and innovative ideas as a safety precaution until they reached the top. Unfortunately, the usual result, after years of repression for the sake of their ambition, is that when the bottle is eventually uncorked there was no fizz. This is the kill chain for soldiers to be versatile, flexible, adaptive, bold, truthful and creative.

Management of change requires cultural review. Culture is an enduring phenomenon that pays a price for change management unless the culture is evolutionary and mindsets agile. Change thus has to be top driven, and bottom-up nurtured. *India's military leadership progression and professional development are culturally weighted in the tactical comfort zone, being essentially embedded in the counter-insurgency/terrorism silos of awards and career progression.* This results in inadequate exposure of its senior leadership in understanding the nuances of operational and strategic domains, thus failure to build a strategic framework that aligns military force application to political intent in war.

Another grey area lies the inter- and intra-service parochialism and cocooned outlook. This retards both applications of combined arms forces and joint warfare focus. To ensure the Joint Force is prepared for the next fight, the need is to graduate from the orthodox PME system based on a single service outdated doctrine to a Joint Professional Military Education (JPME) system keeping pace with overlapping multi-domain operations. While individual service PME institutions need to be reviewed in content and where overlapping integrated, the cross-pollination needs to be enhanced considerably. *JPME must provide extensive experience beyond the just theory and develop leaders capable of rapid collaboration and joint force application moving from interoperability to integrated force dependency*. As part of military diplomacy, the cross-pollination of PME with other countries will keep us attuned to trends in contemporary PME across the globe.

However, pragmatism must not be overlooked while addressing the challenges of induction and management of human resources, operational commitments, budgeting and infrastructure availability. Yet infrastructure development and specialist manning with greater continuity of trainers, both uniformed and civilians, are mandated. Thus the need is to have a sound PME Policy leading to a pragmatic roadmap based on a PME vision with indigenous character.

Proposed PME Policy Contours

Vision Statement. PME must develop future joint warfighters, who think strategically, are empowered intellectually and can creatively apply military power to achieve combat overmatch under disruptive conditions of uncertainty and accelerated rate of change.

Policy Framework. The policy should revolve around the following framework:

(a) Bring clarity to the military dimension for the preservation of national security and its application within the overarching frameworks of multi-domain integrated operations. The learning continuum has to be from strategic awareness for junior leaders to strategic thinking competence for senior leaders.

(b) Foster an integrated joint learning environment and individual service expertise for an in-depth understanding of the future conflict. Jointness cannot be an afterthought that can be bolted on later, in the midst of a crisis.

(c) Strengthen the current curriculum and make it relevant that provides knowledge, skills, and abilities required to perform successfully across a PME continuum from pre-commissioning to retirement at the highest rank in the service.

(d) Create and foster an environment of intellectual growth, healthy professional dissent, risk-taking and creativity. Shun mediocrity and meet aspirations of next-generation officers cadre of Indian Armed Forces.

(e) Shift PME curricula from a predominately topic-based model to an outcomes-based approach and emphasise ingenuity, intellectual application, and military professionalism.
(f) Focus on the seven skills of mastery: Technical and Tactical Mastery, Physical Mastery, Psychological and Cognitive Mastery, Mastery of Military History, Mastery of Leadership and Ethics, Mastery of Operational Art and Mastery of Strategic Thinking.
(g) Focus on the learning curve and military logic rather than competitive assessments and academic evaluation to give freedom of learning and ability of reasoning.
(h) Ensure that a highly qualified, experienced and specialist faculty is maintained in a healthy mix of uniformed, veteran and civil trainers.
(i) As conflicts increasingly become people-oriented, the social and behavioural sciences are becoming important to a military leader who cannot remain isolated from society. Future leaders will need to be well-read and well informed not only in matters military, but also social sciences. Thus, the culture of reading, writing and speaking on a vast variety of subjects beyond the military has increasingly become relevant both in institutionalised education and self-development. Sociology adds value to academic institutions in general and sociological knowledge provides utility in the preparation of future military leaders.

Future PME Construct

The recommended construct for future PME must be cemented around the following:

(a) PME must be synergised with salient aspects of the National Education Policy 2020 where there is an overlap and fusion with civil institutions.
(b) Evolve a PME strategy to right balance training to professional ratio and realign pedagogy commensurate to the service group. The pedagogy needs to be realigned to include more research, group discussions and seminars/webinars.

(c) Synergise academia and technologists with military training as part of the civil-military fusion. Cross-pollination between military, civil, academia and defence industry is desired.
(d) Imbibe combined arms and joint warfare as a professional culture through purple culture and cross-pollination.
(e) Create a pool of specialists both uniformed and civil with continuity. Veterans and think tanks provide a rich resource too which needs to be tapped.
(f) Align HR policy and induction to balance between humanities and social sciences and science. Also, review the dichotomy between the system of assessment and promotion.
(g) Indian Defence University (INDU) is a structural and apex level imperative to meet the requirements of PME. INDU will provide a focused and stable platform for research and standardisation to promote an environment of strategic thinking.

Major Recommendations

There is a need to review, refine and strengthen Professional Military Education objectives, curriculum and methodology at institutions to meet the vision stated earlier. Some recommendations:

(a) *"Democratisation of PME"* to broaden the learning base, not just the top 20 per cent as existing presently. Alongside phasing out the *"Three Tier Education System"* into a continuous decentralised "through life" learning continuum to balance training, education, self-development and career progression. This must form part of the distance learning initiative, imbibing values of self-learning and mentoring at the unit level.
(b) Propagate *"Indian Way of Warfighting, Indian Military History, Geography and Battle Studies"* in the training schedule and research, to draw lessons for the future and imbibe the values of Indian military culture like in Arthashastra.
(c) Develop *"Strategic Awareness Competence"* for junior officers to deal with unconventional warfare, including perils of real-time media coverage, and *"Strategic Thinking Competence"* for senior officers to understand the politico-mil domain of warfare and influence national-level policies.

(d) Promote *"Student Instructor Partnering"* to write professional papers or generate out of box solutions to complex military problems, futures doctrines, lessons of latest conflicts the world over and create incubator spaces to link ideas to outcomes.

(e) Promote *"civil-military fusion"*. There is a need to have a more inclusive faculty with the right mix of civilians and veterans besides serving officers for imparting quality education besides institutionalised interface with eminent civil institutions like IIMs and IITs. Also integrate at SC and HC level courses, PMF/CPO/IPS/IAS/MoD officers as participants in specially designed capsules, for example, JOCAP.

(f) Increase emphasis on *"creativity, risk-taking ability, critical thinking"* and leadership skills to keep pace with the challenges of future warfare.

(g) Invest more in the role of *"technology and multi-domain operations"* as a key enabler in the success of future battle-space. Outsource specialists on subjects like Disruptive Technology, AI, Cyber Warfare, IW, Strategic Leadership, National Security wherein military generalists will not suffice.

(h) Review training curriculum on *"mastering military logic"* and *"knowledge-based decision-oriented leadership"* rather than the "calendar to clock" coverage. Adequate time be given to students for institutionalised self-study and introspection. The *"culture of reading, researching, analysing, writing and speaking on a vast variety of subjects beyond the military, particularly sociology"*, must find greater space both in institutionalised education and self-development.

(i) Enhance the *"tri-service culture and joint warfighting content"* in the scope of military education particularly at the junior and middle levels. Review optimisation of single-service structures where joint institutions can be established and also foster greater tri-service cross-pollination, billeting and tri-service joint training structures. Joint Training Command as a concept must find greater traction.

(j) Institutionalise a specialised capsule for *"Training the Trainer"* rather than on the job training, to bridge the time gap and orient to the training needs. The training infrastructure in keeping with technology also needs an upgrade in keeping with the digital India initiative.

(k) Enhance *"cross-pollination in PME"* with friendly foreign countries and participation in courses like Higher Command. Use the medium of online webinars to foster cross perspectives on matters military besides physical exchanges.

(l) Encourage *"higher education in Indian and Foreign Universities"* in select subjects of national security. This must find focus in the study leave policy which must balance the organisation needs with individual needs.

(m) Encourage *"language skills"* specific to our external and internal security threats especially Mandarin, Urdu and Arabic, and optimise their utilisation without compromising career interests.

(n) Encourage and institutionalise *"self-learning and knowledge enhancement"* through open source online research and institutional support through professional network sharing. Training institutions need to reach out to think tanks like CENJOWS/CLAWS for specific training needs and joint projects.

(o) Create a *"tri-service integrated Faculty of Military"* for orienting strategic level leaders to emerging security challenges, technology interface and role of military power in the overall national security apparatus.

(p) Increase the base for *"Junior Leader training"* at JCO/Senior NCO level by having a Junior Leader Academy at each command with reviewed content to widen the knowledge base. The formation and unit-level training also need greater intellectual fusion and revision in keeping with present operational dynamics.

To Conclude…

PME is the ultimate high ground on which we create and nurture inquisitive, thoughtful and confident leaders to "Think, Fight and Win" future conflicts. The present system is sound yet has not adapted and evolved in its transformation with time. The time is right to align PME as we review modernisation, restructuring, and doctrines. It's time to unlearn and relearn in keeping pace with future challenges for military leadership. Alvin Toffler's reminder must ring a bell, that "if we do not change for the future we shall be compelled to endure it—and that could be worse."

Notes

1. Charles A. Flynn and Lorenzo Ruiz, "Beyond Checkers and Chess", *The Strategy Bridge*, at https://thestrategybridge.org/the-bridge/2017/7/7/beyond-checkers-and-chess-what-juniors-leaders-can-do-to-develop-strategic-thinking
2. Adam Lowther, Brooke Mitchell, Gerard Puccio, and Nathan Schwagler, "Embedding Creativity in Professional Military Education", *The Strategy Bridge*, https://thestrategybridge.org/the-bridge/2020/8/10/embedding-creativity-in-professional-military-education-understanding-creativity-and-its-implementation
3. US Army, "Developing Today's Joint Officers for Tomorrow's Ways of War", at https://www.jcs.mil/Portals/36/Documents/Doctrine/education/jcs_pme_tm_vision.pdf?ver=2020-05-15-102429-817
4. Lt Col DJ Watola, PhD and Allister Macintyre, PhD, "Technology and Leadership: International Perspective", Princeton University, at https://catalog.princeton.edu/catalog/10511171
5. Maj Gen PK Mallick, VSM (Retd.), "PME-An Indian Experience", VIF, September 2017 at https://www.vifindia.org/sites/default/files/Professional-Military-Education-An-Indian-Experience.pdf
6. Lt Gen Atulya Solankey, AVSM, SM, (Retd) "JPME—A Framework to Address the Outcome Deficits", *CENJOWS Journal*, August 2021.
7. Author's interaction at Army War College, December 2021 and feedback from the environment based on an online survey.

Lieutenant General **AB Shivane**, PVSM, AVSM, VSM (Retd), is presently Distinguished Fellow and holding COAS Chair of Excellence at Centre for Land Warfare Studies. A second generation officer is an NDA alumnus, and a highly decorated Armoured Corps officer with over 39 years distinguished military service including a stint in UN mission. As a renowned scholar warrior, he has authored over a hundred publications on national security and geostrategic issues, besides two books and is an internationally renowned speaker. He was the former Strike Corps Commander and Director General Mechanised Forces. The General was a Consultant to the Ministry of Defence (Ordnance Factory Board) from 2018 to 2020.

14

Olive Greens to Corporate and Entrepreneurship

Transitioning to a Second Career

SM Kumar

At 20 years of age, I was leading a team of 44 motivated soldiers in the Indian Army. At 25, I led a team of over 100 specialists operating equipment worth over a hundred million dollars. My peers in civil world, no matter how talented and skilled, handled much lesser responsibilities.

At 40, I hung uniform post command of an active unit. A Commanding Officer (CO) of a battalion (or Captain of a frontline warship) is a very important leader in the armed forces, as is the Chief Executive Officer (CEO) of a corporate entity. I had the privilege to be both.

With nearly a decade and a half as a corporate and entrepreneurial leader, I am convinced that the leadership lessons learnt in the armed forces have served me well in my post-military careers—leadership and followership, goal focus, process-orientation, meticulous planning and attention to details, execution being everything, logistics, project and vendor management, incident and crisis management, team-work, being on time, never taking unscheduled time off duty, camaraderie, esprit-de-corps, communications, and more.

Transitioning out of services can be difficult for over a million servicemen and servicewomen. **Veterans need to transition well—learn, unlearn, relearn, continuously upskill, improve listening skills, develop agility and tolerance for ambiguity**, make an **attitudinal adjustment** to peers and seniors, as well as sharpen their **technology** quotient. Success is sure to come by if we build on our solid foundations.

This chapter has been written primarily with the Indian military audience (looking at a post-uniform career) in mind, but has universal applicability in the context of veterans. I have drawn examples mainly from the Indian context, but have included a few from other countries as well.

The Chapter is laid out in three parts:

I. The new world

II. Transition tips

III. Advice for Entrepreneurs

I. The New World

This section is in three parts:

A. Welcome to the new world; it is different

B. The principles of war, strategy and leadership remain relevant

C. The hard truths

A. The New World

The Primacy of Business

As I hung uniform after a glorious career and re-attired, the new world was markedly different—the vocabulary, the value system, the ethos, as well as the determinants of success. The camaraderie was missing! It appeared more transactional. Here, it was sometimes even OK to talk about your achievements, which took time getting used to.

The atmosphere seemed more relaxed and non-hierarchical, yet professional, efficient and productive. People were on first-name basis (younger colleagues addressed me, and even the CEO, by first name). The structure was lean and diverse (with women, minorities, people from different nationalities and cultures, and a differently abled colleague). It is vitally important for vets to make a quick **attitudinal adjustment** to seniors (some were younger than me) and peers and learn to work in a diverse, non-hierarchical environment.

In the corporate world, **business has primacy**. It is about '**profit & loss**' (P&L). **Cash flow** is important. We need to learn these, and more, in quick time.

The Pace of Technological Disruption is Mind-Boggling

The world is changing rapidly. To put it in context: It took telephone approximately 75 years to reach 50 million users; radio took 38 years, Internet four, and Facebook three years; Instagram and YouTube, WhatsApp and Twitter reached 50 million users in under two years; Angry Birds Space app took 35 days, and Pokemon Go only 19.

Businesses are continuously getting disrupted and new models are evolving. Platform-based business with a strong technology core (asset-light, data-heavy and algorithmically inspired) are gaining ground at the expense of traditional piped business models. With decentralised nature and 'work from anywhere' gaining ground, a trend further accentuated by COVID-19 pandemic, the focus is on remote collaboration, facilitating and enabling teams, leveraging information and technology in unique ways, and consistently adding value to businesses.

The **focus** here is **on business outcomes**. And understanding the business, the customer, the context, the core technology, the ecosystem, critical success factors, and risks is important. Collaboration/synergy with internal and external stakeholders, in pursuit of common mission, vision, values and goals is critical.

Here, adaptability means demonstrating flexibility, agility and the ability to respond to rapidly changing environment and business context, tweaking or changing the business model, reinventing to survive, being resilient, and deftly managing risks.

Add Value; Achieve More with Less

In a corporate environment, you are always under pressure to add value, optimise costs, improve efficiency and productivity, and **do more with less**.

"*As a special force commander, we were asked to pull off near impossible missions with the best trained and equipped troops; here as a Global Chief Risk Officer, I am expected to achieve the mission with a man and a dog...*" This is how a former US Navy Seal officer, confided in me when I asked him how was his new (corporate) world different from his uniformed one? "*Here 'Profit & Loss' trumps*

'Fire & Move' and 'bankruptcy' or 'closing down business' may be preferable over the 'last man, last round' approach or 'never say die' attitude," he added.

'Doing more with less' becomes even more important in an entrepreneurial context.

B. The Principles of War, Strategy and Leadership Remain Relevant

The Principles of War

The principles of war have evolved over centuries, been continually refined, and have acceptance globally.[1] These timeless principles have significant applications in a business environment.

Kings and Generals used these principles to subdue the enemy's will to fight, and to gain territories, taxes, wealth and slaves. CEOs use these principles (with subtle contextual modifications) to win and retain customers and talent, to subdue competition, attain and strengthen market leadership, and multiply the wealth of shareholders. Protecting the 'competitive advantage' of business is akin to having 'moats' around medieval forts.

The first principle of war 'selection and maintenance of aim' has universal applicability. Stephen Covey, in his bestseller *Seven habits of highly effective people* puts it thus: **'begin with the end in mind'**. Similarly, other principles of war, like Concentration, Economy, Flexibility, Surprise, Offensive Action, Adaptability, Reserves and Information have application in the corporate world.

Strategy and Tactics

Many thousand years ago, Sun Tzu wrote "*War is a matter of vital importance to the state, a matter of life and death, the road either to survival or to ruin. Hence, it is imperative that it be thoroughly studied.*"

Sun Tzu highlighted that war was not to be handled through numerical superiority, but by adoption of better strategies and tactics. Winning a war required an accurate assessment of own strengths and weaknesses, as well as those of the enemy, and playing to one's strengths. Sun Tzu also said, "*to win hundred victories in hundred battles is not the acme of skill. To subdue the enemy without fighting is the supreme excellence.*"

The principles of war are applicable to business, management, operations and marketing. The application of principles to higher level planning function is '**strategy**'. Their application to evolve the 'nuts and bolts' of the plan is '**tactics**'.

The missions and methodologies of business are very similar to military—defining the **vision** or purpose, outlining the **mission**, making a **plan**, deducing the **tasks**, designing an **organisation** structure, building a **team** and allocating troops to task, communicating, achieving goals and maintaining momentum. Innovative use of technology and data enhances the efficiency, productivity and chances of success. Risk management and resiliency are important in the corporate context, as in the military environment.

When the principles of war, strategy, tactics and planning are applied to business, successful outcomes are likely.

Leadership and Planning

Leadership is of vital importance in the military as well as in a business context. It is influencing a team to accomplish a mission, by providing purpose, direction, motivation and resources.

Military planning is legendary, not only in wartime but even for routine administrative activities. In military units, even a dinner for guests is planned to the last T. Invitations go out a month in advance, it is personalised, and acceptances and regrets are acknowledged with equal politeness. Who comes in when, is received by whom, and how—is pre-decided. How many drinks would be served, which course of dinner is candlelit, when does the band play, who is toasted and how, what happens post-dinner, how guests are seen off, as well as the thank you notes, and other post-event activities—everything is planned meticulously and executed flawlessly. The contingencies are worked out, and activated as required.

C. The Changed Ground Realities and Hard Truths

The Changed Reality

Remember now you are in the battlefield without the fire or logistic support of the biggest supporting ecosystem and brand called 'the Armed Forces'. So be realistic in your appreciation, estimation, expectation, planning and execution. It's a new world. You are in a new queue. Please shed the attitude of entitlement;

give before you get. Learn to add value and achieve more with less; to listen more and talk less.

The Hard Truth

I meet many veterans who say they are good, and I usually agree with them. Yet, some do not land a good job on leaving (including many with very impressive credentials). To them, my message is this: **Market is a function of demand and supply.** And **there is little linear relationship between being good and landing a job.** So, do not be harsh on yourself, if you do not get a good job immediately. Believe in yourself and your solid foundations. Success is around the corner.

When I hung uniform in 2007, there were hardly any takers for me (despite impressive military and academic credentials), but nearly everyone from Signals (or Communications) branch had more than one job offer from leading global and Indian telecom companies, as the industry was in a high growth phase. Within a year, the Lehman crisis happened, and the market dynamics changed significantly, almost similar to what we are now witnessing with the Covid-induced double whammy of health crisis, economic depression and loss of jobs.

Fail Fast

I hear this term very often from entrepreneurs—fail fast. In rapidly growing, entrepreneurial organisations, failure is not looked down upon. The emphasis is on testing with pilots or proof of concept (PoC), keeping the learning cost low, and find a new and/or better way of doing things, or sometimes even jettisoning the old, for something new and different. This was markedly and refreshingly different from the way I was brought up in a middle-class Indian family where failure was taboo. Similarly, missing a promotion or next rank in the military could mean an end to your ambitions and aspirations.

In an entrepreneurial world, you can fail, and then be remarkably successful. I have interacted with many successful business leaders and entrepreneurs who have bounced back after spectacular failures. Steve Jobs, the legendary Founder of Apple is a case in point. Jayesh Parekh, the Founder of Sony Entertainment Television, an IIT dropout, had a few entrepreneurial setbacks, before Sony happened.

The Good News!

However, there is good news! We operate in a volatile, uncertain, complex and ambiguous (VUCA) world—such an environment provides fertile ground for military leaders to excel.

A Colonel or General ahead of our name still probably gets us that little extra respect. We have a duty to use the goodwill capital wisely.

And we have solid foundations, good network and tangible assets (as well as intangible ones); we can build on these.

II. Tips/Advice for Transition to a Corporate Career

When Should You Hang Uniform?

I hung uniform at the peak of my career on the last day of command of my unit (the one where I was commissioned and spent the bulk of my life), when career-wise things were looking very bright for me. This decision surprised many, including my family, colleagues and dear ones.

Inevitably, I often get asked one of these questions—why did you take premature retirement? Or, when should one leave the armed forces? To the second question, the answer is simple—on superannuation. Because, the armed forces are probably the best organisation that you will ever get to serve in.

Decision to leave the armed forces is a very personal choice, and often an emotion-filled one! While most will, and should, leave on superannuation, some may wish to leave prematurely. Supersession or non-fulfilment, or having to address other personal priorities in life, could be among the reasons for opting out. I personally feel that one should leave prematurely only, if and when, your motivation begins to dip, and you still have enough juice left to make a mark outside. "*Leave when people ask you WHY, and not when they begin to ask why not.*"

However, irrespective of when you decide to leave, and when the organisation lets you go, the more important aspect that I wish to highlight is this—"**hanging uniform does not mean that your association with the armed forces has ended.**" We continue to benefit throughout our lives from our association with armed forces—whether it be directly in terms of pensions and benefits, or more intangibly in terms of societal standing, solid foundations, and more. So, we have an obligation and duty to pay back, which can take multiple forms—giving jobs to veterans or assisting them or their families, innovations to support the defence of your nation, promoting veteran entrepreneurs, assisting in nation-building in other ways, including volunteering and mentoring the youth, or assuming a coveted office like a Vice Chancellor, or leading union or state public service commissions, or task force or in a rare case, a constitutional appointment like a Governor.

One must prepare well for the transition to a second career. While transitioning, we need to build networks, learn about opportunities, job applications, resumes, certifications, networks that promote veterans, and companies that have veteran-friendly policies. We need to build on our solid foundations, learn, unlearn, upskill and reinvent ourselves.

Bring Your Competence and Passion Along

Please bring your competence and passion along; leave your ego behind. Think BIG while firmly remaining rooted in ground realities, remain committed to excellence, be driven by passion, and focused on success.

Carry Military's core learnings with you. After hanging uniform, I had the good fortune to attend a six-months' programme at IIM Calcutta. Later on, I was invited to IIMs, FTI and MDI to share my learnings with armed forces officers transitioning to a second career. I was quite surprised to discover (sometimes) a misplaced emphasis on blanking out all military learning and then starting with a clean slate. Just to be doubly sure, I also exchanged notes with some other accomplished veterans who had either been invited for similar interactions, including one of the co-authors of the book, and this is what we concluded, "**without the core learnings of the military, the veterans will lose their value and great edge. We need to build on our solid foundations** (as indeed the whole corporate edifice, strategy and tactics is built on military fundamentals) in terms of skills, as well as ethics and values—that is going to be the recipe for success. Failure to do so can have disastrous consequences." Of course, we need to embrace new technologies and concepts, adopt newer approaches and ways of working, unlearn a few things and learn new ones (as the world is continuously evolving). Whether we go on to become a Governor or a CEO or an entrepreneur, military learnings will continue to remain very useful and relevant.

Transition is a Process—Approach with Military Precision

Transition is a process. Approach it with military precision. Remember, in the military, when you had to plan an operation, you spent a huge amount of time and effort gaining relevant information—enemy as well as own, did a detailed objective analysis, troops to task, war-gamed plans endlessly, built contingencies, paid meticulous attention to details; and then after making an excellent plan, you focused on executing it flawlessly. Please **approach your career transition** with the same **rigour and passion.** Do not just make CVs listing out all your credentials, forward them to a dozen military and veteran friends, and think it is done. Success in transition will be proportional to the amount of focused effort and passion.

Make Yourself Easy to Find

It's a big, chaotic world outside. Make yourself easy to find. Position yourself closer to opportunities. In your military life, camouflage, concealment and confidentiality were virtues. Not so during the transition. You have to **make yourself searchable** and/or easy to find. Speak at forums in areas of your expertise, network, keep your LinkedIn and other digital profiles updated, and they must contain keywords.

Choose Your Career Wisely

The first fundamental question most veterans are confronted with is what career will best suit them. In my experience, **career choice is a function of** (in decreasing order of priority):

- **Market.** A function of **demand** and **supply.** Go for what is in or likely to be in demand.
- **Passion.** What excites you? It is specific to You.
- **Skills.** Your employer will eventually pay you for your skills and deliverables.

Do Not Rule Out Any Course of Action *Ab Initio*

Carry out a military-like appreciation—do not rule out any career option. Finding a corporate job is not the only option before you. Depending on when you hang uniform (in 30s, 40s or 50s) and your specific context, you could choose to pick up a job, be self-employed, become an entrepreneur, write a book or memoirs, become a social leader, run a charity or not-for-profit, administer your housing society, or retreat to your village or hills. You could lead a skill development programme, a school or college, or hold a public or constitutional office.

Follow Your Passion

Get into a career that you are passionate about—one that gives you meaning, fulfilment, happiness, sustenance and longevity.

Career transition would not be linear or orderly. Have patience. Believe in yourself.

Retain a positive attitude and outlook. Resilience is important—there will be lows! You will bounce back.

Upgrade your skills. Embrace technology. Be a lifelong learner.

Once you have decided on what career to opt for, the next challenge is to convince the employer/recruiter to hire you. And if you embark on self-employment, remember, the learning cost could be steep (and that would often involve considerable financial risk).

Strengthen Your Network

Network is Net Worth. Jobs or opportunities may come from referrals. Expand your network. Remember, the best **networkers give more than they get.** You could begin by networking with veterans who are doing well in second or third careers. In India, there are a number of platforms (like Soldier2ndLife by Brisk Olive, Forces Network, and Military to Corporate) where you get useful advice about career transition. Some companies promoted by veterans (like MitKat Advisory) also help mentor and prepare veterans for a second career. A start-up in India, Humfauji Initiatives advises veterans about post-retirement financial planning.

Ecosystem is Important. Invest in relationships; invest in ecosystems. Strengthen your digital network—update your **LinkedIn** profile—align it with your new career goals.

Know Headhunters. To reach any of the 330 million Hindu Gods or Goddesses or deities, you have to go through a temple priest. Headhunters play an important role in connecting you with potential employers and helping you bridge or circumnavigate the few skill gaps that you may have.

Find a Good Mentor. A good mentor is extremely important. Find a mentor who understands your context and potential, as well as the outside world.

Meet in a Non-Interview Environment

Position yourself well. Preferably **meet in a non-interview environment,** and **control the narrative.** Talk about relevant and transferable skills, and use data and statistics. When appearing for a position in logistics, talk about your logistics experiences. I loved the infantry officer who described moving a special train thus—"I carried out a multi-modal, incident-free move of 1,000 men and 20,000 tons of material over 4,000 km over two days and three nights."

Listening Is Important. Remember, communication is more about listening. It's one thing many veterans are really bad at. Vets are used to listening very hierarchically. If you don't listen carefully, you will miss out on important clues.

In the pandemic world of online interactions, technological set-up, knowledge of platforms, having apt backgrounds and pre-testing is important.

Vocabulary is Important

The corporate vocabulary is different. Besides, each industry has its own set of jargon. Here, P&L, top line and bottom line are important. The terms 'hunter' and 'farmer' have specific meaning for sales professionals.

Numbers carry greater credibility than statements. Try to quantify your accomplishments and explain in the form of a story which is easily comprehensible. Talk in language that corporate leaders understand. Remember, if you were a gunner or a cavalier, you not only fired shells or rockets or missiles; you also led teams, did an analysis of competition (enemy), planned, coordinated, monitored, course-corrected, and achieved results. Your work involved great team work (among the crew). You also oversaw operations and maintenance of equipment.

Use terms which resonate with the interviewer and are relevant to the job at hand. When talking about a corporate security position, speak about intel, surveillance, liaison, perimeter security, cyber security (cloud, data, endpoint, network, application security, policy and processes) people, vehicle and material management, security budgeting, emergency response, business continuity, resilience, crisis management, command centre operations, travel security, executive protection, event security, project management, loss prevention, SOPs, etc. Also demonstrate your understanding of the business-relevance and strategic understanding by saying something like "I will endeavour to make security less human-dependent, more business-relevant, intel-led, tech-enabled, cost-conscious offering better (bang for the buck or) return on investment."

Humans have Biases; You may be Misunderstood

Appreciate that humans have biases, and that you may be misunderstood. Most civilians respect the military, but are not really sure what the soldiers do in peacetime, or what skills and relevant experience they bring to the corporate world. Understand that employers may have biases about you being hierarchical, rigid, not used to listening, low on initiative, and used to following orders, etc. Give comfort to recruiters that you are not egoistic, but intelligent, agile, goal-focused and open to learning. Give them comfort that while you may take a little time to learn, you will do so quickly, bring your other valuable, transferable life skills into play, and will get things done.

Why should Companies Hire Veterans

The best piece of advice on this subject was offered by **President Barack Obama** who tweeted: *"To every CEO in America: If you want someone who will get the job done and done right, hire a veteran."*

Veterans bring invaluable skills and competencies, are quick to learn, good at multi-tasking, and excellent at taking ownership, and getting things done. While looking to hire veterans, it may be a good idea to have at least one veteran on the selection panel. Look for the skills that may be transferable—leadership, management, goal-focus, process orientation, meticulous planning and attention to details, operational excellence, logistics, projects, HR, admin, security and crisis management, as well as specialist technological skills. Look for attitude, learnability passion and will to succeed. Remember, most of the guys who have left prematurely want to do more with life, and would be great assets to your organisation. What you need to teach them is business-focus, profit and loss, and data-driven decision-making. What vets need to demonstrate is quick results, strong sense of ownership, energy and passion, and quick attitudinal adjustment to seniors and peers.

Employers need to understand that veterans hang uniform in different service brackets (short service officers usually after 10 years, some regular commission officers after 20 years, and most after superannuation)—they bring varied skills and competencies. Please understand their capabilities (and may be some limitations) to employ them suitably.

Veterans excel in crisis situations. These are extraordinary times, and veterans are worth their weight in gold. Remember, veterans excel in crisis management. Military leaders understand that during a crisis, their job is to lead from the front, over-communicate, keep teams focused, engaged, away from distractions, with morale and motivation high, and their well-being looked after. Veteran leaders also understand that crisis impacts different people in different ways, and find new and innovative formulae to get the best out of everyone.

Companies have Veteran-Centric Programmes

Many companies, particularly the global multi-national companies (MNCs), have programmes specifically directed at veterans—these include Amazon, Bank of America, Microsoft, GE, Accenture, etc. Some universities and B-schools like Harvard Business School and Indian School of Business (ISB) welcome veterans for the skills and diversity they bring to the programmes. Indian entities of MNCs like Goldman Sachs run special veteran-focused programmes. There are specific opportunities for women officers in MNCs, as promoting diversity and hiring veterans is often a consideration for their human resources (HR) departments and business leaders. In Indian Armed Forces, Director General Resettlement (DGR) facilitates professional courses with leading B-Schools, and Army Welfare Placement Organisation (AWPO) helps in the corporate placement of veterans (particularly NCOs, JCOs and WOs).

My Advice to Those Who Leave in Star Ranks

Firstly, many Congratulations on reaching where you did! It is so difficult to get there in a pyramidal organisation, with so many bright, hard-working professionals, through one of the fairest selection systems. You are obviously bright and competent, and have been privileged to envision and executed at a scale, in complex environments, which very few of your counterparts in the civil world can dream of.

"Continue to do and behave like a General (or Air Marshal or Admiral). Dream big, do big." Play to your strengths—the choice of what you can do is limited by your imagination. Now is the time (to prove to yourself) that your Reporting Managers who graded you 9 in 'tolerance for ambiguity'[2] over each of the last 30 annual confidential reports (ACRs) were right.

Not all of you will become a Governor (like one of the authors of this book), but each of you can make a difference. A few of you could get together and lead a movement to plant a million trees, or support a dozen entrepreneurs from India's leading technology and management institutes or AITs or AIMs or HDMC, or build a university for cyber security or defence innovations, or for futuristic learning, or establish a think tank to promote India as the new regional and/or emerging global power, or support a social cause like building old age homes. Think 'Out of the Box', carry out a military-like appreciation, war-game your ideas and plans, and implement, sustain and continually improve it with military-like precision. Keep the flag of the Indian Nation and the Indian Armed Forces flying high.

III. Advice for Entrepreneurs

I have been an entrepreneur for over a decade; during the journey, I have tasted significant success and experienced monumental failures—I learnt a lot from my failures.

Every entrepreneur's story is different. Enumerated below are my hard-won learnings as a first-generation veteran entrepreneur.[3]

Entrepreneurship involves a fundamental mismatch between resources and ambition. Entrepreneurs start with big dreams, but very few resources. It is important that the dreams do not become small, just because they have fewer resources. The size of the idea is important.

Have a powerful idea ... be distinct or extinct ... differentiate or die. Entrepreneurs must think exponentially, not incrementally.

The Why is important. Entrepreneurship is different from self-employment (which is essentially about you). **Entrepreneurship must have a value and**

purpose beyond making you rich and famous. It must be pursuing a cause that attracts other talented, capable professionals. The mantra for success is not money, market conditions or team alone, though they have some part. It is the WHY that is very important.

Platform-based models. Identify a big enough problem; look at future-focused, tech-enabled, platform-based scalable models. The world over, piped business models are giving way to platform-based start-ups. Amazon, Alibaba and Flipkart disrupted traditional retailers. Uber, Lyft, Ola and AllMiles are revolutionising transport. Netflix has redefined entertainment. In China, Tencent, Baidu and ByteDance symbolise this shift. Airbnb and Oyo scale up faster than Marriotts and Taj Hotels. We also need to build agile ecosystems.

Do not be afraid of failure (though culturally, in India, it is easier said than done). We have failed more often than we have succeeded. Behind every two YES has been eight NOs. But, fail fast. And after a failure, bounce back, hard and strong.

Focus ... do less to do more ... Do not do more than one thing at a time. I often hear wannabe entrepreneurs saying... I am doing this... and this... and this... and at least one of them will succeed. The sad truth is—none will. If you do one thing that you are truly passionate about, your chances of success magnify.

People, people, people. Great co-founders (chemistry among them is most important) are vital to entrepreneurial success. If you can surround yourself with people who believe in your idea and you (and not those who work only because they need a job and pay cheques), you will do well. **Surround yourself with people brighter and smarter than you**—that's the best way to grow. Do not be insecure in their company. Each of the heavyweights brings a set of values, the sum total of which is more than the individual aggregate.

Let go! Delegate. The graveyards of the world are full of people who thought they were indispensable.

Cash is queen. Keep a close track of cash flows and collections. **Top line is vanity, bottom line is sanity, cash is reality.**

The rule of three. Whatever you plan will take three times more money, resources and time.

Go with your gut. Do not have paralysis due to over-analysis.

Your plan will not survive contact with the market. Yet **planning is inevitable** and you must plan meticulously. Seek the advice of more experienced entrepreneurs.

Create champions and success stories; celebrate wins.

Sound ethics makes great business sense. Get the culture right from the beginning. Set the tone from the top. There must be a fair distribution of rewards and risks. We have been generous with sweat equity.

There is **no right or wrong age to be an entrepreneur.** Steve Jobs, Bill Gates and Mark Zuckerburg started very early; the founder of Kentucky Fried Chicken (KFC) started after 60. **Passion has no age.**

Handle pressure. Pressure on entrepreneurs to succeed and scale up is so intense. Please handle it. Do not come under peer pressure. There have been highly publicised cases of entrepreneurs committing suicide and succumbing to pressure.

Conclusion

Veterans have it in them to succeed in their post-uniform careers, and examples of successful transitions abound. But remember, you are entering a new world, with different rules of the game. Carefully select the second career—it should be a function of market, passions and skills.

Veterans have solid foundations. This paper provides tips for early and successful transition, including highlighting the need for unlearning, learning, upskilling, networking, understanding business and P&L, and need for attitudinal adjustment.

Military and entrepreneurship are both high-risk vocations—Veterans make excellent entrepreneurs. The last section recounts the learnings of a veteran entrepreneur.

Remember, it all begins with the first principle of war. And there is no substitute for meticulous planning, flawless execution and making use of opportunities.

To the companies looking to hire veterans, I would remind you of what President Obama tweeted, *"To every CEO in America: If you want someone who will get the job done and done right, hire a veteran."*

Wishing all veterans a great second (and subsequent) career! Many of us who have gone through the journey would be privileged and happy to share our experiences and help you realise your potential.

Afterword

Through my three and half decades of military, corporate and entrepreneurial innings, I have had the honour of leading great teams, of being led by some great leaders and seeing some great ones emerge, particularly when the chips were down. As a leader, our job was always to envision, empower and energise our teams.

My teams and I have been through many a crisis; together we came out victorious. A key learning has been the need to build great teams, and let them flourish in a great organisational culture. We worked hard to select people not only with skills, but those with great attitude, shared values, learnability and ability to adapt to the organisational culture.

It has been a huge honour to lead men and women of mettle. They have contributed in great measure to our modest success. To my teammates of 9 Mech Inf (7 Grenadiers), Mahindra SSG and MitKat Advisory, all organisations with great culture, values, ethics and people—heartfelt gratitude and thank you!

And to the veterans looking for a second career—build on your strong fundamentals; dream big; do big. Jai Hind!

Notes

1. Principles of war were formally codified by Carl von Clausewitz, a Prussian General. Peter Drucker, management guru and author, endorses Clausewitz's views.
2. In armed forces, "tolerance for ambiguity" is a *(very important) quality for an officer in his ACR. One needs to be continuously rated outstanding (or near outstanding in *qualities like Integrity, tolerance for ambiguity, etc.) to be considered worthy of making it to the highest ranks.
3. The author's entrepreneurial learnings (with MitKat Advisory, a platform-based Asian Risk Consultancy Leader), formally codified as "MitKat Mantras" have been covered in a book *Success from being Mad* by RS Sidhu.

15

Military Leadership

The Way Forward

AK Singh and Anil Sengar

Introduction

The armed forces have always been vital to the nation's security and well-being, and remain even more so in the 21st century. How this instrument of last resort performs will be determined by a number of factors, both tangible and intangible, but to a large extent by the leadership that steers the organisation in peace and leads it in war.

While this book has covered various nuances of military leadership at the strategic, operational and tactical levels, this concluding chapter will examine the overall leadership climate and analyse whether it has kept pace with the challenges of the 21st century. We shall aim to recommend pragmatic, systemic changes to improve the leadership climate, that will produce leaders who will measure up to the highest standards of military ethos.

So let us start by forcefully stating that the Indian Armed Forces are a most professional and well-led organisation, in fact, the pride of our nation. Being so important to the nation's well-being, there cannot be any scope for complacency. Others may have this luxury, the armed forces do not.[1] They need to constantly look within to remain dynamic and relevant, always one step ahead of the threats and challenges that confront them over the horizon. This chapter is an attempt to do the same.

Part I. The Leadership Climate–Honestly Speaking

Military Ethos

The armed forces face a very challenging environment, which is likely to get even more complex in the future. Added to this are the challenges faced by the human resource, linked to the dynamics of society. It is, therefore, necessary to understand and reflect on the military ethos and values that provide the basic foundation on which the armed forces function.

Ethos is defined as a core set of attitudes and values that give an identity to a person, community or organisation. In Greek, ethos means custom or character; it also encompasses ethics, principles and morals, a sort of accepted personal or organisational benchmarks that provide the guiding light even amongst the darkest clouds. The defining character of the Indian Armed Forces is built upon an intrinsic value-based system. Over the years a certain amount of diffusion may have set in, that needs correction and the values reinforced.

Core Values

The value system which forms the bedrock of the military ethos is composed of the basic sense of "service before self". Here we will examine the three core values that lie at the heart of the military ethos of the Indian Armed Forces, and which need to be zealously guarded and reinforced.

- **Apolitical.** The armed forces as an institution do not have any political preference, but serve the constitution of the country and take legitimate orders from the government of the day. Over the years there have been sporadic incidents, where some in the senior hierarchy may have crossed a line, but the organisation as a whole has stood firm and true to this core value. In an era of increasing political expediency, the apolitical character of the armed forces needs to be preserved in the face of any inducements or short-term considerations.
- Universally, the political leadership spins narratives to shape public (mis) perceptions to suit their agenda or conceal reality and setbacks. Where the military leadership joins the political chorus, national embarrassment can't be far away. We have seen the experience of the US in Vietnam, Iraq and now in Afghanistan, where the writing was on the wall but was given

a different spin by the senior military hierarchy. It is imperative that the military leadership maintains integrity in their statements for the national good and its own image, within and outside the military. The festering Ladakh face-off 2020-2021, amply reinforced this necessity. Military leadership will do well to remember that in an era of prying media and intrusive technology, truth is their only ally, except when a certain narrative is temporarily engineered for a specific operational purpose.

- **Secular.** The forces live together, train together and fight shoulder to shoulder, without any consideration of religion, region, caste or creed. In an era of greater polarisation in society, the armed forces stand as a beacon of harmony, earning the trust of all citizens.
- **Professional.** When many institutions in the country are in decay, the forces reflect very high levels of professionalism and equally high standards of personal and professional integrity, in the true spirit of their military ethos. There are aberrations, but these need to be capped firmly and not allowed to grow. There can be no other way.

Character of a Successful Military Organisation

The character of a successful military organisation is made up and forged by a number of tangible and intangible factors and attributes. We have picked four of these, which define the character of the forces more than any other.

- **Leadership.** The Indian Armed Forces boast of outstanding leadership, which gives them the edge in any conflict. However, this great asset and force multiplier, is in some ways also the Achilles heel, which if not nurtured within a conducive environment, can prove detrimental to the organisation's effectiveness. This has been adequately covered in earlier chapters. Suffice to summarise that while there may not be a crisis, the trust and bonds within various levels in the organisation need to be constantly reinforced to optimise the effectiveness of the organisation. The way forward to invigorate the leadership is discussed later in this chapter.
- **Authority-Responsibility-Accountability.** This is a key essence of the armed forces and distinguishes them from other organisations on the civil side, where this linkage is rarely if ever established. While the forces are good at establishing personal accountability, they have fallen short in establishing professional accountability for serious lapses in peace and

conflict; Kargil, Uri, Pulwama and now Ladakh to name a few. While the organisation should have broad shoulders to absorb genuine errors in the line of duty, acts of omission and commission based on gross incompetence or neglect need to be brought to book, specially at the senior level, where it could mean the difference between life and death, victory or defeat.

- **The Warrior Ethos.** The Chetwode Motto: "The country first, the men you command come next, your own ease, comfort and safety, come last always and every time", has been the guiding light for the military leadership, but is it enough? Or a supplementary code has become necessary. The warrior ethos of the US Army states: "I will always place the mission first, I will never accept defeat, I will never quit and I will never leave a fallen comrade". The US Army has worked to instil this warrior ethos in all soldiers by the way they train, live and fight. For the Indian Armed Forces, the Bhagavad Gita shows the way forward: "I am a warrior, fighting is my dharma. I will train my mind, body and spirit to fight ... always protect the weak ... and embrace the consequences ...". A detailed ethical code has also become necessary to guide rank and file in light of the falling standards in our society and prevent a grey zone from flourishing.
- **Regimental System.** The regimental system is the bedrock on which the armed forces, specially the Indian Army functions. Regimentation has been used by many armies as a most effective tool to exercise control over the soldiers, to enhance their battle-worthiness and fighting spirit. Post-independence, the Indian Army adopted the existing regimental system based on class/regions and later brought in the mixed class composition in keeping with our constitution.
- In conflict situations, apart from the National Spirit, it is this Regimental Spirit that reflects the Izzat (honour) of the unit/regiment that motivates the soldiers to achieve the seemingly impossible. The exceptional acts of bravery shown by 2/Lt Arun Khetrapal in 1971 and Capt Vikram Batra during the Kargil conflict stand testimony to this. A grateful nation bestowed its highest honour, posthumously, on both these gallant warriors. So let us remain sensitive and reinforce this unique system that is so intrinsically linked to the well-being and battle-worthiness of the army. The Navy and Air force too, though to a lesser extent, follow in spirit and derive great motivation from their affiliation with the ships and squadrons.

In the same vein, it is important to highlight the dangers of misplaced regimentation, in what may be termed tribal loyalty, causing serious damage to the ethos of the army. The quote below aptly sums it up:

"The forest was shrinking, but the trees kept voting for the axe because its handle was made from wood, and they thought it was one of them."

Decoding the Leadership Climate

"I am not afraid of an army of lions led by a sheep. I am afraid of an army of sheep led by a lion."

—Alexander the Great

The term 'Leadership or Organisational Climate' encompasses a wide range of aspects relating to the leader, the led, the organisation and the environment. It also encompasses the intangibles that could make or mar an organisation.

It was the end of Day 1 of a test match between Australia and Bangladesh. Batting first, Bangladesh were 355 for six wickets. Their Captain, addressing the press conference expressed his satisfaction at the score but stated that they needed another 100 runs to be safe in the match. Later, Australians were struggling at 155 for six in the first innings. When asked, how he saw their position in the match, the Australian Captain said, we certainly are in a tight spot, but we got to figure out how to win from here. Australia won the match.

A leadership climate is the 'pot pourri', of the tangibles and the intangibles that either create self-belief of invincibility or of self–doubt in an organisation. The leadership sets the pace by creating an enabling environment of trust and growth where every individual sees himself as a warrior in his own right. Important aspects of a good leadership climate are: a culture of nurturing future-ready leaders at all levels, team spirit and a winning attitude, where everyone is prepared to subjugate personal interest for the larger good. A good leadership climate is characterised by a culture of trust and collective ownership. It is about We and not Me.

Climate refers to the long-term. Thus, for a good leadership climate to sustain, it has to rest on the pillars of military values and ethics. The culture of leadership development ensures that ethos and values are internalised and sustained effortlessly through generations and crises. Functionally, it sets the guidelines for decision-making and conduct, and generates momentum as the decision-making is pushed to an appropriate lower level.

The onus of creating a good leadership climate rests squarely on the leader. The quickest way to vitiate the environment is by giving precedence to personal orientation over the team's interests.

The professional US Army hit rock bottom in the Vietnam War. It was a leadership climate at its worst. Incongruity in the stated and practised military values broke the military cohesion and trust at every level. Deceit and lies to its people in collusion with politicians, killing civilians in the numbers game, the My Lai massacre, islands of luxury in the rear when troops were suffering heavy casualties at the front, different duration of tenures for officers and men, etc. The troops saw far too many officers of doubtful integrity leading them. There were more than 700 cases of fragging against the officers in Vietnam.

In the Second World War, in the German Army, 220 generals out of 660 died in combat and maintained its cohesion till the end, while the US army lost 40 out of 1,100 Generals and not all in combat. The Israeli army is another fine example of a good leadership climate. In the famous raid on Entebbe to secure the release of hostages in Uganda, only one soldier died: the mission leader Lt Colonel Netanyahu. **In the German Army, character was one of the most important bases for the selection of a military officer, which was never diluted, despite depleting numbers.**

The leadership climate will dictate the effectiveness of any army in the long run. It is also the ultimate judgment on the quality of leadership. The leadership of the Indian Armed Forces have stood the litmus test except for the 1962 Indo-China conflict, always leading from the front and by example. This needs to be preserved in letter and spirit.

Crisis in Military Leadership: Myth or Reality

> *"How many Generals know what they stand for, and more important, what they should stand up to?"*

A leader is not judged by what he makes of himself. He is judged by what he makes of the task and the people he is responsible for, by the lasting legacy he leaves behind. By the same analogy, subordinates are also the best judge of leaders who lead them, hence the relevance of perceptions.

There are three distinct levels of leadership in the military. Starting with the tactical at the unit and brigade level, the operational leadership at the division and corps level and the most critical, the strategic level, which includes the Army Commanders and Chiefs, as also the PSOs (Principal Staff Officers). Distinct as they are, each level is positively or negatively impacted by the leadership climate above and even below.

Our experiences on the borders have demonstrated that the distinction between the levels of leadership has got diffused. A tactical situation in Eastern Ladakh snowballed into a strategic one. This points towards introspection of our leadership training at all levels. Broadly speaking, there is little to complain against the leadership climate at the unit level, barring exceptions, where there was a clear, but temporary shortfall in leadership.

In the 1962 Indo-China conflict, there was widespread failure of leadership, specially at the strategic and operational levels, barring individual exceptions. This failure and the redemption in 1971 have been covered in separate chapters earlier in this book. Closer in time, the military leadership has earned itself a mixed reputation both in peace and conflict.

There is a growing perception that the senior hierarchy, at least in some cases, does not fully measure up to expectations, and has fallen short in securing the genuine interests of the armed forces. This is also the result of increasing transparency and awareness in rank and file, as also an intrusive media. It also points to a certain lack of effective communication to mould perceptions based on facts.

What is it in the environment that it continues to throw up some leaders who fail to inspire and live up to the time-tested leadership ethos under the three pillars—Character, Competence and Commitment. The deficit of intellectualism and professional military education required to deliver at the highest level has been evident for some time, and this is further compounded by a growing mismatch between soaring ambitions and limited abilities. A chapter has been devoted to this important subject in this book.

More worrisome is the fact that few of those who reach high ranks have managed to get through the filtered layers of the same system without their character and professional flaws being noticed. In the light of the above, the system of selection and promotion to higher ranks needs a deeper analysis.

The present system reduces a military leader to decimal points and the third decimal point decides who gets promoted and who does not and who is approved for command and who for staff. The personality element of the command, so essential in the military, has been somewhat diluted. While the system was introduced with the aim to remove biases, it has revealed a number of shortcomings, specially in selection to senior ranks. Many correctives have been applied over the years, but maybe, a different approach is now warranted.

Does our leadership climate stretch the commanders professionally through positive turbulence or penalising for incompetence adequately? How important is the 360-degree input in getting a true picture of an officer? The civil bureaucracy has already adopted this 360-degree input, it's time for the armed forces to give it a closer look.

Visionary and Transformational Leadership

A dispassionate review of the trends in dealing with external and internal challenges points towards the inadequacy of strategic vision and failure to foresee the challenges before they hit us. The 'monotonously' excessive focus on counter-insurgency/proxy war, with attendant HR spin-offs, is also affecting the growth of a vibrant senior military leadership. The military mind needs to also stop thinking of itself only in terms of 'a last resort option', but to rediscover the utility of force, not only to win wars, but also how to avert them without compromising our national interests.

In summary, the following assessment may not be too far off the mark as far as senior leadership is concerned:

- A small percentage are outstanding military leaders, with clarity and conviction, well versed in the higher direction of war.
- A fewer still qualify to be role models based on their integrity, competence and commitment.
- A percentage of mediocrity manages to get in and is not able to rise above the tactical level.
- The status quo approach and turf considerations manage to retain a hold on some at the cost of the organisation.

While there may not be any crisis in military leadership, a shortfall in 'visionary and transformational leadership' to measure up to 21st-century challenges becomes apparent and needs attention.

Part II. The Way Forward

"There is a saying that the obvious need not be stated".

The Indian military is proud of its legacy since independence. We have had our setbacks in the Indo-China War 1962 and Sri Lanka 1987, the reasons for which go beyond the military doorstep and are too well documented to be repeated. The Indian Armed Forces set glowing examples in the Indo-Pak War, 1971 and the Kargil War. The Kargil War was amongst the toughest battles fought in the history of warfare. This was yet again reinforced in the Ladakh face-off with the Chinese. The above notwithstanding, there are significant shortcomings of leadership at various levels that must be examined and correctives applied where necessary.

Let us start with the most critical aspect of national security:

Civil-Military Relationship

India faces multiple security and developmental challenges. **'Incredible India' needs to become 'Invincible India'** which is more relevant in the larger context.

The wars of the last few decades have demonstrated the complexity of concepts such as the notion of victory, conflict termination objectives, the difficulties of achieving strategic victory and the post-war complexities, etc. The complexities and lack of an exit strategy came out loud and clear in the US withdrawal from Afghanistan, as we too experienced in Sri Lanka. Post the terrorist attack on our parliament, the Indian military mobilised for 'Op Parakram' without being given clear politico-strategic objectives. The military, thus, was left to navigate the complexity without a lighthouse. As a result, there are no benchmarks to define the gains from this initiative.

Modern conflict is more likely to manifest in the form of political/foreign policy contests interspersed with military episodes. Force is more likely to facilitate political settlements, rather than fashion outright military victory.

So what we need today, more than ever, is for strategic organs of the state to harmonise; only then can incredible India become invincible India.

The politico-bureaucratic leadership needs to be sensitised to the nuances of 'matters military'. On their part, the higher military leadership needs to comprehend the dynamics and challenges of national governance. They need to develop the tact and the skills to deal with the government, to meet national security objectives in a tight fiscal and democratic environment.

Rank and Leadership Equation

An organisation like the military can easily become a victim of its own straitjacketed character. In the military, the authority of an officer is mostly defined by the ranks. There is a tendency to see ranks as synonymous with leadership, which is not the case and needs to be understood.

Rank is an official position of authority that in the armed forces is earned through a competitive process in senior ranks. With higher ranks come enhanced responsibility, authority and related accountability for the organisation, the mission and the men under command. Leadership, on the other hand, is not only a responsibility related to rank but is more a moral authority that comes without seeking, when a person wins the trust of his command. What differentiates a commander from a leader is whether his command follows him because they have to or because they want to.

Mission accomplishment needs ownership, commitment, credibility and trust. It is primarily the leadership element that sows the seeds of extreme ownership and trust and not the authority of command. Rank, therefore, does not always equate to leadership, a tendency to do so is not uncommon. The leadership of Hav Ishar Singh at Saragarhi, 1897, Maj Shaitan Singh at Rezang La, 1962, Maj Gen Sagat Singh at Nathu La, 1967, Gen Sam Manekshaw as the Army Chief in the 1971 War and the junior leadership in Kargil, 1999, highlight the primacy of the man over the rank. This applies equally at all levels, from the tactical to the operational and even strategic levels. While all three levels of leadership are important, it is the quality of operational and strategic leadership that sets the stage and direction for the rest. Addressing this level should remain the immediate priority in the context of the fragile international, regional and internal security environment.

Improving the Leadership Climate

We now come to the crux; to make pragmatic recommendations to address the shortfalls as perceived. Let us summarise the main contours of effective Generalship at the highest level.

- The BE—It is about the man. In simple terms, it is the unimpeachable character that does not waver either in the face of temptation, threat or when there is a price to pay.
- The KNOW—It is about the competence to deliver at the highest level. It essentially involves *Vision, Phronesis* (practical wisdom) and *the Edge* (30,000 feet view and the ability to take tough decisions) to keep the organisation future-ready.
- The DO—It is about managing change; ensuring that the changes within outpace the changes in the outside environment. An important aspect is navigating the bureaucratic-politico minefield in a democratic nation like ours.

Reinforcing Value-Based Leadership

> *"Character is the key to all ethical issues: take care of Character, the rest will take care of itself."*

Both the houses of our parliament have an ethics committee to monitor and enforce ethical conduct by the lawmakers. Similarly, there is a code of ethics for civil services. Military values clearly lay down the guidelines for ethical conduct, yet the demonstrated ethical standards, in some cases, fall short of expectations.

This is a very serious issue. How do we ensure an ethical leadership climate? **Good ethical conduct is driven either by conscience or through the deterrence of severe punishment.**

Where do we begin? It is sometimes opined that the academies do not change your character. You go as you come. Thus, the importance of the Services Selection Board (SSB) comes into sharp focus. The SSB system was adopted from the British in 1948 and continues to be archaic and rigid. Its selection is focused on picking up error-averse middle-of-the-road candidates, rejecting anyone with unorthodox/out-of-the-box views. A change in the whole approach is long overdue.

The case of Late Col Ashutosh Sharma, Commanding Officer, 21 Rashtriya Rifles (RR) [The Guards] gives a reason for introspection. Throughout his service, he was an excellent military leader. He served three tenures with 21 RR as a volunteer. As the Commanding Officer, he made the supreme sacrifice leading an operation. He was awarded the Sena Medal, three times. Well, the intriguing part is that he was rejected by the SSB twelve times and made it in the final attempt for OTA before he ran out of age. Something simply does not add up.

The academy is the cradle of leadership. The prime aim must be to nurture a rookie cadet into a soldier of character and conscience, who internalises the military values. Unfortunately, the survival dictum of '*Beg, Borrow or Steal*' militates against the officer code. Thus, the leadership and ethical culture in the academies needs a serious review, to be in congruence with the stated code—I shall not lie, steal or cheat or allow others to do so. The right foundation at this critical stage is of utmost importance if leaders are to live by the highest military ethos. This has been elaborated on in a separate chapter.

The following are worth considering:

- A credible methodology of 'integrity and ethical audit', where considered necessary.
- To recognise and reward officers of proven ethical and integrity credentials. Punish and weed out officers with proven ethical and integrity deficiencies from the promotion process.
- Protect the whistleblower when the report is correct. Punish him when it is ill-intentioned.

Ethical conduct needs repeated reiteration right from the academies and compliance ensured through deterrent punishment to demonstrate zero tolerance. ARTRAC could consider designing dynamic capsules on military ethics for different courses of instruction and different service brackets. Formation based seminars/webinars should be conducted periodically by the commanders personally. Why the commanders personally? This will compel the borderline officers to self-correct their course, for it would be very embarrassing to not practise what you preach. Perks and privileges in India are a legacy of the colonial era. The British themselves have different standards as there should be.

In 2019, Captain Nick Cooke Priest, the Captain of the British aircraft carrier was removed from command of the battleship for using his official car for personal use on a Sunday, even though he paid for the fuel.

The above example shows that military ethics are absolute with no scope for greyness or personal discretion. **There is a requirement to clearly lay down the ethical code that leaves no doubt on the red lines.**

Climate of Growth and Optimism

> *"Commander's first objective is to be continually prepared for war. Second to create an environment in which every man finds personal meaning and fulfilment. It is only the attainment of the second that will ensure the first."*
>
> —Anonymous

Transparency and Fairness. It is important that the organisation is, and also perceived to be, transparent and fair. Those who make it, perceive it to be fair, those left behind fuel the perception of unfairness. The truth lies somewhere in-between, with biases coming into play in select cases. While the selection system may be called fair and acceptable, it's the grading and performance appraisal system where biases and aberrations creep in, leading to disillusionment and negativity.

Recognition and Awards. When General Krishna Rao retired as the chief, the only award he had was a PVSM earned as a divisional commander during the 1971 War. Today, every second Lt General (including one of the editors) has four awards for essentially distinguished service in various ranks. There is a need to review the award policy in its entirety to restore their value and share the recognition. Maybe an embargo of no more than two distinguished awards may be considered.

An environment of Trust and Ownership. The organisation must reinforce an environment of trust and ownership and have a trustworthy mechanism where subordinates can express their grievances. When men stop bringing their problems to you because they either believe that you are incapable of solving them or you do not care, is the lowest point of the leadership climate.

Professional Dissent. Genuine and constructive professional dissent needs to be encouraged in the armed forces since its exclusion would only encourage mediocrity and predictability. **Let's be clear that blind conformation is not loyalty, nor independent thinking, dissent.**

Work from 'Hope of Success' rather than 'Fear of Failure'. There are grounds for thinking that incompetent commanders tend to be those in whom the need to avoid failure exceeds the urge to succeed. The armed forces need to reinforce an environment where leaders focus on success rather than failure avoidance.

Professional Accountability. This is an essential requirement to promote a culture of professional excellence. Unless we do so, the incident-free mediocre commander will outshine a risk-taking commander who might falter.

Optimising the Human Resource

Human resource optimisation is a function of the tangibles and the intangibles. The tangible relates to training and hardware and the intangible relates to cognitive skills and his human quotient, i.e. the intensity of desire and pride in getting the job done.

Human Quotient (HQ). It is the ultimate judgment on the effectiveness of an organisation. It is a combined function of leadership, self-esteem, training and purpose. Different aspects that affect HQ have been addressed in other parts of this article. Here we are highlighting the most critical aspects.

Professional Culture. The armed forces, like most other organisations, are being subsumed by powerpoint culture, event management and expediency. Every military activity should be done with a purpose to the desired professional standards, devoid of bull.

- You train on the ground as you will fight in battle.
- Man is the most precious resource. Every man-hour should be purposefully utilised.
- Anything that does not add professional value must be cut out.
- Excellence is a habit born out of a culture of excellence.
- Merit should be the most significant basis of growth.

Yodha Ethos. The most powerful tool any military leader carries is not his weapon but his mind. The Indian armed forces must reinforce with vigour the "yodha ethos" and develop "scholar warriors", who have the character and courage of conviction, combined with professional competence, mental agility and strength, to measure up to the challenges of the 21st century.

Professional Military Education (PME)

It is incredible that at one stage the Military History paper was removed from the entrance examination of Staff College. It took ten years to reintroduce it.

Do the present system and the leadership development address the changing dynamics? The complexity of warfare also demands perception of the intangibles, these cannot be taught. A senior officer must develop a broad-based intellect as he goes up in his career. The complexity and multidimensional character of warfare demand multidisciplinary competencies. A leadership programme to train officers in operational art and various facets of the higher direction of war has now become imperative. We believe that the Army Training Command (ARTRAC) has established such a faculty of Leadership in the Army War College. We strongly wish to emphasise the criticality of the quality of the faculty. The visiting faculty consisting of eminent, proven and charismatic military and civil leaders, both serving and retired should be based on role model leaders, irrespective of rank/status. It will be worthwhile to nominate an advisory board headed by the Army Commander to steer this wing.

Keeping in view the importance of PME, a separate chapter has been devoted to this aspect in the book.

Harmonising the Aspirations with the Vision and Goals of the Armed Forces

Every individual in the military is a package of unique emotions, aspirations and personal obligations.

It would be pertinent to start by highlighting that the Indian military has the worst career satisfaction ratio amongst all government services. About 60 per cent of officers get superseded in the very first promotion board at the early age of 35-37 years to live a de-motivated existence for the next two decades. **Supersession is a big blow to the self-esteem of most officers and families. The armed forces can ill afford such a high percentage of disillusioned officer corps.**

For the military to be operationally effective, it is important to harmonise the aspirations of its human resource with the organisational vision and goals. Let us briefly look at the aspirations of the environment today.

- An enabling environment of growth that meets their self-esteem and self-actualisation needs.
- An organisational culture based on military values where the senior leadership takes ownership by setting a personal example.
- A transparent and just organisation that honours merit, and also provides honourable avenues for those who do not make the cut.
- A value-driven higher leadership that can ensure that genuine concerns of the military are addressed by the government.
- Fair and just treatment of the military in terms of status and pay parity in consonance with other government services.
- Comprehensive defence policy for the country so that the military gets the direction and support for a purposeful transformation and capability development.
- Basic materialistic needs such as good accommodation and schooling, which remains a cause of mental stress across ranks even today, despite some worthwhile initiatives taken by the organisation. More remains to be done.

While some of the above aspirations can be met within the organisation's ambit, others will require the consideration of the government. The hierarchy must assert and convince the political authority of their case.

Harmonising Abilities with Ambition. It is unflattering but true that a large number join the military today for a job and not a passionate vocation. In the course that passed out from IMA in June 2021, there were only nine officers' children. The choice of arms in the academy too is guided by where the prospects of promotion to higher ranks are better. This is clearly putting the cart before the horse. Good grading in courses has become a single-minded mission and not learning, as it opens the way to UN Missions. The skewed focus and ambition beyond abilities is a disruptive recipe, given the steep promotion pyramid. This does not augur well for the well-being of the organisation and needs to be addressed.

By the end of the tenth year of service, the career trajectory of an officer becomes fairly clear based on his performance. To start with, make officers aware of the environmental realities, where they stand, developing the right attitude and providing opportunities for alternative growth options. A similar exercise can be undertaken in higher ranks to diffuse unrealistic expectations and guide such officers to alternate avenues and empowerment for a second career. Talented and qualified officers in IT, cyber, space, weapon technology, finance, procurement, intelligence, etc. could be given opportunities for specialisation that meets the organisation's and their self-actualisation needs.

Promotion to Higher Ranks. There is a saying that the armed forces are as good as its Generals/Admirals/Air Marshals are. The dynamics of the promotion system in the present avatar needs some improvement to enhance its credibility.

It is **'one-man-centric'**, depends largely on who serves under whom and where, lacking in consistency, with periodic flip-flops, which open it to accusations of bias.

Admiral Arun Prakash, former Chief of the Naval Staff, wrote an article, *In response to Mohan Guruswamy's article on the Indian military being 'incompetent', dated August 6, 2016.* On the issue of the all-important report by the Chiefs on General Officers, he wrote, "Like other reporting officers, the chief too, must provide full justification, via written remarks, for overruling the earlier grading(s). Given the fact that the Chief has the power to change relative ACR rankings, thus the merit, it becomes incumbent for holders of this highest office to be transparent and without any bias."

Over-assessment in confidential reports of which most are guilty, has overwhelmed the system, making it lose its discerning character. In this melee of inflationary reporting, the organisation loses out on some professionally competent officers with high integrity and ethical values. Similar is the case of appointments at senior levels, with square pegs being driven into round holes. It deserves deeper examination.

- **Pro-rata System.** The current pro-rata policy in HC/HDMC/NDC course nominations and promotions to Brigadier rank devalues meritocracy. ACR as the major basis of selection/promotion has serious shortcomings as highlighted earlier. There is a need to inject credibility and 'scholar warrior content' by introducing a new format to assess the officer's suitability for higher ranks, based on a broad syllabus of the higher direction of war. This should have a certain weightage in drawing out merit.

- To ensure minimum acceptable standards, there is a need to establish a **bench-mark** below which officers are not nominated to career courses or promoted just because of arm-based vacancies. These vacancies should then be allotted to other arms based on merit.
- **Review assessment system.** The assessing/reviewing officers should be able to offer a true representation of officers' performance and **potential for the roles he is expected to play in future.** Notwithstanding the operational deployment of the Indian army, the vast majority in command assignments are assessed on peacetime deliverance. Even in operational deployments on the Line of Control and Counter-Insurgency, there rarely are challenges that test a formation commander's professional acumen as would conventional operations. The challenge, therefore, is to identify and select commanders from a non-combat environment who will deliver in combat.
- **Assessment of integrity. The ACR as a certification of character and integrity does not pass muster.** Virtually everyone is getting an outstanding report, quantified as '9', thus, permitting officers with questionable professional competence and integrity to get through and surprise the system in the senior ranks.
- **Resurrecting the 'Spoken Reputation' and Reinforcing 'Value Judgment'.** We could examine introducing a 30-minute interview by a board of five members, comprising three service officers and two HR academicians of repute to assess relative suitability for promotion as an independent input. We strongly believe that spoken reputation **through peer rating in the promotion board agenda and 360 degree reporting on character and integrity** for Value Judgment merits serious consideration.
- **Command/Staff Selection.** Ours is a **command-oriented Army;** yet everyone is not suited for it, and many unsuitable officers are given crucial command assignments. This is a most critical issue and needs a more dynamic solution.

Selection of the Service Chiefs

Beyond the rank of Maj Generals, promotions are based on the date of birth. Once an officer is promoted to Lt General, he will go on to become the Chief purely on the basis of age. This defies logic. All army commanders are neither equally competent nor suited for the role of the Chief. The highest appointment charged with national security must be based on seniority-cum-merit. The perplexing question is how, by whom and on what basis is the merit evaluated at that stage.

The government should always have the last word. However, there is a widespread perception that over the years, the selection of service chiefs have not validated the justifications on which competent officers were superseded. Where they followed seniority, it was not always the best man for the most important job.

Both the nation and the services are equal stakeholders. It is therefore desirable that the government gets professional 360-degree feedback on the candidates under consideration for service chiefs. A high-powered board consisting of the Raksha Mantri, CDS, Cabinet Secretary and NSA may be constituted, and all examinations placed on file. The whole purpose should be to select the best man for this critical appointment, in a transparent manner.

The dilemma with selecting Generals/Admirals/Air Marshals is:

> "Not everything that counts can be graded and not everything that can be graded counts."

Conclusion

The Indian military has always risen to the challenges. Its professionalism, ethos and selfless service have earned the gratitude and the respect of the nation. We are into an era where unpredictability is the new normal and the change is happening at a rapid pace. The hostile regional and the complex global environment dictates that, as a nation, we constantly assess-reassess-modify our doctrines and capabilities and keep ourselves ready to respond to the challenges.

The military is a complex organisation. It comprises tangibles and intangibles that shape its character and effectiveness. The fact is that every link in the chain, however innocuous, plays an important role and cannot be ignored.

In this concluding chapter of the book, it has been our effort to focus on the critical aspects of military leadership and organisational effectiveness, highlight the shortcomings and make pragmatic and systemic recommendations to improve the grey areas.

The quality of leadership, organisational climate, values and ethics, meritocracy, perception of fairness, all contribute to the operational effectiveness of the military.

The military serves in a dynamic environment. The security challenges, both internal and external are constantly evolving and the character of warfare rapidly changing. Thus, for the military, change is an ongoing work in progress. It needs leadership with vision and foresight and synergy of all stakeholders to stay ahead of the challenges. Managing change starts with the timely realisation of what is changing in the contextual environment and harmonising it with the changes in the organisation. **For the military to remain future-ready, the pace of change within must outpace the pace of change outside.**

Often ignored is the most important aspect of human resource. It is the maintenance of the human spirit that wins wars and not just the effectiveness of weapons or organisational structures. As our analysis suggests, we need to take a serious note of human resource issues that have been highlighted. It is important to remember that, whatever be the magnitude of the campaign, it all boils down to small teams of men being led by a brave and competent leader in those circumstances. They are the most important weapons of war.

The Indian military is at the cusp of transformation with the establishment of the Chief of Defence Staff, the Department of Military Affairs and integrated theatres (to follow), in a security environment of complexity and uncertainty. Such a transformation not only needs the due diligence and perception of the intangibles on the long-term consequences on the part of the military, but it also needs all organs of the state and the military to function as a well-knit team. There is far too much at stake; meeting the deadline cannot come at the cost of getting it right.

Effective promotion methodology remains at the heart of military effectiveness. A dynamic approach is required to ensure that the best are selected. The US has tried one such methodology using best HR practices with excellent dividends. It included cognitive and psychological assessments, creativity, ethical leadership, ability to develop subordinates, etc. A comprehensive process, it culminated in a 30-minute double-blind interview by a board (that also included NCOs as advisors for selection of battalion commanders), while ensuring that a board member walked out if he knew the interviewee candidate. We understand the Military Secretary's Branch is studying this report. We strongly recommend that enabling provisions be suitably co-opted to eliminate present shortcomings and subjectivity. The details are covered in the article titled *Reinventing the Leader Selection Process* by Everett Spain. It can be accessed on this link.

https://hbr.org/2020/11/reinventing-the-leader-selection-process

Why is this system so necessary? In the US experiment, 34 per cent of officers who were recommended by the board, would not have made it in the conventional method. In the exit survey, over 96 per cent of officers voted this as the better way to select future commanders.

The army is all about top down-top first. We fix this part and the rest will take care of itself. We can only ignore these issues at our own peril.

"A visionary leader makes changes when they seem unnecessary to most. For, when you start changing when they seem necessary, you have long missed the bus. The days of the wisdom, 'why fix it when it ain't broke, are long passé."

References

1. Lt Gen AK Singh and Lt Gen VK Ahluwalia, *Military Leadership in the 21 Century* (New Delhi: KW Publishers, 2019).
2. Warrior Ethos as described on the US Army Values site.
3. Maj Gen Yash Mor, "Scholar Warrior Ethos of Indian Army", SP's Land Forces, issue 6, New Delhi, 2020.
4. Lt Gen AK Singh, "Lt General Hanut Singh, MVC", Memorial Lecture, 2016.
5. Maj Gen Anil Sengar, "The Be-Know-Do of Generalship".
6. Lt Gen HS Panag, "An Assessment of Military Leadership", at https://timesofindia.indiatimes.com/blogs/shootingstraight/an-assessment-of-military-leadership/

Index